BIZARRE CRIMES

Bizarre Crimes

DASTARDLY DEEDS, DEVIOUS
SCHEMES, BUMBLING BURGLARS,
& OTHER FOOLISH FELONS

JOE RHATIGAN

imagine!
Publishing

An Imagine Book

Published by Charlesbridge

85 Main Street, Watertown, MA 02472

(617) 926-0329

www.charlesbridge.com

Text and illustrations copyright © 2011 by Charlesbridge Publishing, Inc.

All rights reserved. Printed in China, November 2011.

Library of Congress Cataloging-in-Publication Data is available on request

2 4 6 8 10 9 7 5 3 1

For information about custom editions, special sales,

premium and corporate purchases, please contact

Charlesbridge Publishing at specialsales@charlesbridge.com

CONTENTS

CRiME ANd MERRiMENT

None of us is perfect. That in itself is a major part of what makes us human. However, some are slightly less perfect than the rest of us, and thus more human. These "more human" people do bizarre and illegal things and—best of all—they get caught doing them. And then their exploits end up in newspapers, on television, and on YouTube. They urinate in stupid places. They discipline their children with car-wash hoses, or let their drunk children drive them home because they, themselves, are too drunk to drive. They call the cops, or dial 9-1-1 to ask where to buy drugs. Oh, the humanity!

Another part of our humanness is our innate ability to laugh at others; to chuckle, giggle, and guffaw at silly people doing stupid things. Why do we feel such joy at others' all-too-human predicaments? This book won't try to answer that question, but it will certainly aid and abet you in the laughter department. *Bizarre Crimes* is chock-full of amazingly stupid crimes that people committed and then were caught doing. So, until you get snagged doing something bizarre and illegal, enjoy this book. Laugh at the silly criminals doing stupid things! Snicker at the bad Santas, the ego-driven celebrities and sports stars, the awful moms and dads, and more. Hey, you're only human.

RiDiCULOUS ROBBERiES, NOT-SO-CLEVER CRIMES

With 24-7 news, Facebook, Twitter, and more, we've all become a bit obsessed with (and perhaps tired of) giggling babies, ticklish animals, celebrity wardrobe malfunctions, and oddballs committing stupid crimes. So consider yourself lucky that I spent days and days combing the interwebs for the ridiculous crime stories you *haven't* heard a thousand times or heard about a thousand different criminals committing. Because really, how bizarre is it if everybody's doing it? So, cow tipping, which is so last century, is out. However, tipping fiberglass art cows is totally now.

The Young and the Lawless

A Covington, Louisiana, man arrived home one day to find three young children burglarizing his house. How young? Two of the suspects were six and the other was three. They made off with two hammers, a box of fudge, a Candy Land game, some money, cigarettes, and a jar of vegetables. Police officers arrived at the scene to find the children playing across the street. When they approached,

one of the six-year-olds pulled out what looked like a handgun and placed it on the ground. (It turned out to be a BB gun, but still . . .) The boys were too young to be arrested; however, their mother could face charges. She wasn't home at the time of the crime. She was attending a parenting class. (Perhaps she can get a refund.)

Left at the Scene of the Crime

If you decide on a life of crime, you should treat crime scenes the same way forest rangers ask us to leave forests. One of the tenets of good forest maintenance is to "leave no trace." These days, the good guys can nab you if you lick a stamp or drop a skin cell on the way out the door after a robbery. However, you don't need to be as obvious as these clueless crooks you're about to meet. The CSI folks love taking out the big equipment, so don't ruin it for them by making it quite so easy to catch you.

➔ A nineteen-year-old man forced his way into a home, intent on robbing it. One of the two occupants of the home punched the crook. He fled the scene without his gold teeth, which had fallen out after the punch. Minutes later, the crook's mother went to the home to pick up the teeth.

➔ A twenty-five-year-old man and an accomplice broke into a home, struggled with the occupants, and made off with some jewelry and a wallet. However, as they made their hasty getaway, a vital piece of evidence fell out of their car: a black T-shirt with a picture of one of the crooks on it. The slogan on the shirt read, "Making Money Is My Thang." He turned himself in two days later.

➔ A man who held up someone in the parking lot of a Subway sandwich shop had just filled out a job application at the restaurant. The victim recognized the eighteen-year-old man from inside the Subway, and police used the application to obtain the suspect's home address. The Homestead police chief said of the criminal, "This isn't regular criminal behavior. He's not a rocket scientist, but this one takes the cake."

➔ A man in Gallatin, Tennessee, tried on a pair of jeans at the local Walmart and left without taking them off or paying for them. Luckily for police, the man left his old jeans behind in the dressing room, his wallet still in the back pocket. Police caught the man later on after running out of a LongHorn Steakhouse without paying the bill.

→ Three women in Springfield, Missouri, did the ol' dine-and-dash at the local Waffle House, leaving behind the unpaid $39 check . . . and their purses. One of the women returned and demanded the purses. The manager told her to wait—the cops would be there any minute.

→ A man was caught on video driving up to a gas station, breaking a window, and stealing cigarettes from the store. The video also shows the car's license plate falling off as the crook drove away.

→ A Calgary, Canada, thief left his résumé in the stolen car he abandoned. However, police have yet to find the man.

→ A man handed a note to a bank teller demanding $20, $50, and $100 bills. Unfortunately for the robber, he wrote the note on his pay stub. Sure, he took the time to cross out his address with a marker, but investigators could still read it when they held the paper under the light. The Philadelphia man was arrested shortly after the holdup.

Virtual Theft

In 2008, two Dutch teenagers were convicted of beating up a classmate and stealing items from him. They were both sentenced to more than 150 hours of community service. The catch here, though, is that the classmate was never touched, nor was anything physically taken from him. The three teens were playing the multiplayer online game RuneScape, and the internet bullies virtually roughed up their classmate and stole virtual stuff from him. Doesn't matter. The Dutch court ruled that "virtual goods are goods (under Dutch law), so this is theft."

Meanwhile, also in Holland, a teenager was arrested for stealing online furniture in the social networking game Habbo Hotel. The teen was accused of stealing more than $5,000 worth of virtual merchandise as well as hacking into other people's accounts.

Moo-ving Violations

Drunk college kids love cow tipping! Just ask the residents of Burlington, Vermont, who dealt with a rash of cow sculpture tippings in 2010. The fiberglass cows were part of a community art project where businesses bought the cows, decorated them, and then showcased them in front of their stores. Six of the six-hundred-pound sculptures were tipped, and four men were arrested for the vandalism, including one man who ended up in the hospital when the cow he was tipping (decorated as a French waiter, complete with tuxedo, black beret, and pencil-thin mustache) fell on his foot, breaking it in three places.

Twilight Dimwit

A fifteen-year-old girl who told authorities that the bite marks on her body came from someone who attacked her while she was jogging was charged with filing a false report. When deputies couldn't find any other evidence of an attack, they pressed the girl for the truth, and she finally admitted that the bites came from *Twilight*-inspired vampire role-playing she was doing with a nineteen-year-old man. The two had engaged in "fantasy biting," and the girl made up the story because she was worried her mother would freak out when she saw the bite marks.

Oops, Wrong Car

A man, after robbing a bank in Rouen, France, jumped into a police car and shouted, "Get away quick before the cops come!" He had apparently run into the wrong car.

Crime Ring Flushed Out

Shelby County, Tennessee, sheriffs arrested two men for stealing brass toilet fittings from the men's rooms of several area retail stores, including Target, Schnucks, Wendy's, and Kroger. A local legal expert said, "These guys are what is the worst part of Memphis. Memphis has so many good things, but we do have the dumbest criminals."

Getting a Handle on Crime

A Wisconsin man was arrested for a crime spree in which he stole dozens of doorknobs from construction sites. The man admitted that he is obsessed with doorknobs and would often steal a variety of items from different sites "so that it would look like a typical burglary rather than someone just stealing doorknobs."

The Geezer Bandit

The FBI has been searching for an elderly man who is suspected of robbing at least thirteen banks in California. They say he usually wears a cap, glasses, and a sweater or blazer. He sometimes has an oxygen tank or a cane with him, but he never leaves the house without his gun. Since they haven't been able to identify the elderly man so far, the FBI is entertaining the thought that the man is wearing an elaborate mask.

The Polite Robber

"Polite robber" may seem like an oxymoron, but one holdup artist comes as close to polite as anyone holding a gun on you could possibly be. After grabbing a cup of coffee at a convenience store in Seattle, Washington, the bad guy approached the counter, paid, and then, while the cash register was open, pulled out a gun and asked, "Could you do me a favor? Could you empty the till for me, please, and put it right here? I am robbing you, sir." Notice the use of *sir*. How respectful! What manners! After a little back and forth, the man continued: "I really am sorry to have to do this, but I've got kids . . ." A heartfelt apology always feels good after delivering bad news. "Thank you very much, and I really do appreciate it. If I ever get back on my feet again, sir, I'll bring it back." One should always thank a service person after robbing them. It's only polite.

Seattle authorities arrested a sixty-five-year-old man in connection to this crime and charged him with armed robbery and forgery. "Sorry, sir, and thanks for not wearing a mask. It was really easy to identify you on the surveillance cameras. Have a nice day."

Fishy Behavior

A British man walked into a pet store and convinced one of the employees to sell him a goldfish and put it in a drinking glass he had brought with him. And sure enough, while a friend caught the action on film, the man proceeded to swallow the fish. Police arrested the man on animal cruelty charges after the video appeared on Facebook.

Kitty Litter

A woman from Coventry, England, was caught on video petting a cat and then grabbing it by the scruff of its neck and throwing it into a garbage can. (Yes, she closed the lid.) The cat's owner posted the video on YouTube in order to catch the cruel kitty criminal, and she was eventually identified and arrested. Meanwhile, the video went viral, and the woman received death threats and now has Facebook "hate" pages to contend with. "[She's] worse than Hitler," someone posted on one of the pages. The woman didn't help her cause when she said she thought everyone was blowing the incident out of proportion. "I don't know what the fuss is about. It's just a cat." She also told reporters that as she was petting the cat she thought "it would be funny" to put it in the bin.

I'm Confessin'

A rapper who goes by the name G. Dep (short for "Ghetto Dependent") and once worked for Sean Combs's record label was feeling bad about a robbery he committed years before, so he walked into the 25th precinct in Harlem, New York, to confess to shooting a man three times in the chest. The rapper, however, didn't think the man had died. But he had, and G. Dep was charged with murder and held without bail. In a jailhouse interview with a newspaper reporter, the young man said, "I was surprised—for some reason, I really didn't think that he died. When they told me, I was like, 'Oh, I'm not going home after this.'" And he didn't—he faces life in prison if found guilty.

Blind Justice

Police in Jackson, Mississippi, pulled over a car that was weaving through traffic. What was the cause of the erratic driving? Was the driver drunk? No, the passenger was. In fact, the passenger was too drunk to drive home, which is why he enlisted his blind friend to drive instead.

Yield to the Lord

A woman in Northampton, Massachusetts, was cited in 2010 for failing to yield to a pedestrian in a crosswalk after she ran into a man. He was taken to the hospital for facial injuries. Nothing bizarre here . . . except for the victim's name: Lord Jesus Christ. No word yet on whether or not Christ has forgiven her.

Buttered Up

A man and woman in Sicily, Italy, thought they had committed the perfect murder. Unfortunately, they left some butter behind. The plan had been to tie up the woman's ex-husband, stuff a big ol' slab of butter down his throat, watch him suffocate, and wait for the "murder weapon" to melt before the police arrived. Everything went according to plan, and the police even initially bought their story of the ex-husband having to be tied up because he had shown up at their home drunk and attacked them, but then suddenly collapsed and died. Unfortunately for the lovebirds, forensics experts found remains of the deadly butter in the dead man's airways.

Life and Then Some

A man from Tuscaloosa, Alabama, is currently serving out his ten-thousand-year jail term for murdering his wife, mother-in-law, and a random college student. Meanwhile, when an Oklahoma rapist/kidnapper/crook appealed his 2,200-year jail sentence, he received a new trial, was quickly convicted again, and had an additional ninety centuries added to his current sentence. In a bit of good news, the Court of Criminal Appeals dismissed part of the case, and the man's sentence was reduced . . . by five hundred years. He can now be released as early as the year 12,744.

Not-So-Smartphone

A motorist in Boise, Idaho, reported being pulled over by a man who didn't look like a police officer. The driver said he had pulled over when he saw the familiar flashing blue and red lights from the car behind him, but the "police" car briefly stopped and then drove away. The suspicious motorist followed the dubious police car and called the real cops. Police located the questionable car and arrested a twenty-one-year-old Idaho man and charged him with unlawful exercise of the function of police. What did the guy do? He used a cell phone app that flashes blue and red to pull over cars, just for fun.

Manicure Mayhem

A forty-four-year-old woman was put behind bars briefly for calling 9-1-1 four times. The emergency? She wasn't satisfied with the length of her nails after a manicure. During one of her calls, she stated, "I'm just calling the police because something happened up here at the nail shop. This woman put her hands on me first, okay."

Double Trouble

A forty-three-year-old man from Avon Park, Florida, was charged with fraudulent impersonation, altering a public record, passing a forged-altered instrument, and several misdemeanors after being pulled over by police and then pretending to be his twin brother. The sheriff who pulled the man over initially charged the twin with DUI, and deputies didn't discover that the man had signed his brother's name on his citation and jail forms until the following day. The twin said he did it because his license had already been suspended.

Hot Cars, Cold Crimes

Winters in Toronto, Canada, are often harsh, as was the crime spree that affected affluent suburban neighborhoods from 2003 until 2005. This is how the crimes went down: A cold rich person starts his or her expensive car and then returns to the house until the car warms up. Car thieves, prowling the neighborhood looking for $80,000 SUVs with their motors running, get in the toasty cars and drive off. Easy peasy. It's like taking candy from a baby—a very rich baby. Police warned residents to remain in their cars while they warm up. "Unfortunately, that's the best thing you can do," said one detective.

Pranks Gone Wrong

Practical jokes, though often funny, are almost always one step away from getting somebody really hurt and/or arrested. Here are some that took that extra step.

➜ A man who posted a fake video on YouTube of himself singing a lewd song in front of a classroom full of kids was facing up to twenty years in jail on child pornography charges. All he really did was play an appropriate song in front of the kids and then later splice in footage of himself singing the inappropriate song. He pleaded guilty to a lesser charge and had to spend two months in jail. That and he cannot be within five hundred feet of a child under the age of seventeen.

→ A twelve-year-old Ohio boy was charged with assault after leaving a pencil upright in the seat next to him at choir practice. You can guess what happened next, but I'll fill you in anyway: A kid sat down and the pencil penetrated about four inches into the kid's left butt cheek. Ouch.

→ A twenty-one-year-old Milwaukee, Wisconsin, man thought it would be funny to don a ski mask and pretend to rob his mother as she came home from shopping. A very surprised mom pulled a .357 Magnum from the waistband of her pants and shot her kid in the groin.

Pissed Off

A California State University, Northridge professor has been charged with two misdemeanor counts of urinating in a public place. The charges stem from videotape of the professor peeing on a colleague's office door. College officials had set up a hidden camera after "suspicious puddles" were found near the colleague's door. The camera then caught the pissed-off professor in the act. A university spokesperson said, "We will not be releasing the surveillance tape." Thank goodness for that.

FAST-FOOD FELONIES

To be honest here, this chapter wasn't in the outline I submitted to the publisher. In fact, I had no idea so many awesomely bizarre crimes took place in fast-food restaurant chains until I started researching this book. The crimes occur on both sides of the cash register, and sometimes in the drive-thru as well. And for some reason, you can see many of them on YouTube. No fast-food chain is exempt, and any of the hundreds of food items available at these fine establishments is capable of setting off a riot. So perhaps you should consider warming up that leftover pizza instead of stopping at the local Denny's the next time you want a quick bite to eat.

The Burger Bully

A thirty-one-year-old woman on spring break in Panama City Beach, Florida, attacked employees of a Burger King. She jumped on the counter, threw whatever she could get her hands on at employees, pulled a manager's hair, and more . . . all while wearing a bikini. (And, of course, all caught on video and posted on YouTube.) Why? She felt her food order was taking too long. She told police, "We tore the Burger King up. I don't play no games." Neither do the police, who arrested the woman and charged her with misdemeanor battery. The attacker also noted, "If I knew what was gonna happen, I would've gone to Taco Bell."

IN OTHER NEWS: A man in Orlando, Florida, also unhappy with how long his food was taking at a Denny's, fired three shots outside the restaurant. He fled the scene without his order, but was tracked down and arrested by police.

The Wendy's Whack Job

A woman from Daytona Beach, Florida, (what is it with all these Floridian fast-food felons?) faces charges of aggravated assault with a deadly weapon after chasing a Wendy's employee around the restaurant with a stun gun. The woman, angry at the drive-thru service, got out of her car and entered the restaurant, stun gun a-blazing.

The Fresh Fries Felon

Police were called to a McDonald's near Sandusky, Ohio, when a man refused to accept the fries he was given because they had been sitting under the heating lamp and weren't fresh. The customer refused to leave until he got fresh fries. One employee either threatened the man with a mop or actually hit him with it—reports vary.

Au Naturel

An Ontario, Canada, man is facing charges of public indecency after arriving naked at several fast-food drive-thru windows. In one incident, he arrived at the drive-thru window of an A&W with two other nude men in the car. An employee described in her testimony feeling "very uncomfortable" and said that "the driver was trying to pretend he was getting a wallet out of his back pocket, which made his private parts go back and forth on his leg."

The Hero Zeroes

Two Domino's Pizza workers, each in their thirties (so they should have known better), were arrested in Conover, North Carolina, for distributing prohibited foods. Why were the foods they were distributing "prohibited"? Well, the man and woman posted a YouTube video of one of them making a "Special Italian Sandwich" by stuffing cheese up his nose and then placing it on the sandwich, farting on the salami, and sneezing on the food. The two were arrested once their video went viral, attracting millions of views before being taken down. The video from Domino's CEO Patrick Doyle saying that the store had been completely sanitized "top to bottom" not surprisingly didn't receive as many views. Doyle also said, "We're reexamining all of our hiring practices to make sure that people like this don't make it into our stores." Good idea.

The McNugget Mauler

A Toledo, Ohio, woman was arrested and served sixty days in jail for punching two McDonald's employees and then throwing a bottle at and shattering a glass window. The intoxicated customer was angry that the restaurant wasn't serving Chicken McNuggets because they didn't serve the tasty chicken treat for breakfast.

McCrazypants

After moving to a just-opened cashier at a busy McDonald's in Athens, Georgia, two women were yelled at by an angry woman who threatened to kill them for jumping in line in front of her. The angry woman then left the restaurant, but later on attempted to keep her promise as the two women made their way to their car. She pulled out of her spot and attempted to run them over. Both were struck but not seriously wounded.

Hash Burgers

Three employees at a Los Lunas, New Mexico, Burger King were arrested after lacing burgers with marijuana and then selling them to two police officers. The cops didn't notice the pot on the meat until they had eaten about half of their burgers. After confirming the substance was marijuana, they went to the hospital for evaluations. "It gives a whole new meaning to the word 'Whopper,'" said the officer's attorney. The cops are suing Burger King for an undisclosed amount.

The Kentucky-Fried Frolickers

Three seventeen-year-old employees at a KFC in Anderson, California, were fired when they posted photos of themselves on MySpace turning the restaurant's industrial-sized sink into their own personal hot tub. The photos show the girls in bikinis and underwear frolicking in the sink. They may have been inspired by a twenty-five-year-old Burger King employee in Xenia, Ohio, who, a few months earlier, had posted a four-minute video of himself taking a bath in the restaurant's sink—*au naturel*—while several other employees, including a manager, looked on.

The Taco Bell-ter

A thirty-one-year-old man in Fairbanks, Alaska, was arrested and sentenced to one day in jail after hitting the manager of a Taco Bell in the face with a Double Decker Taco. The man said he threw the taco because he believed someone had spit in it.

Fire in the Hole

For the last three or four years, an illegal prank on fast-food employees has become a YouTube phenomenon. It's called "fire in the hole," and basically, an idiot drives up to a fast-food drive-thru window and throws something (usually the drink or shake he or she just purchased) at the employee while yelling, "Fire in the hole!" In North Huntingdon, Pennsylvania, police arrested four teens for throwing a liquid containing hot sauce at a Subway employee. They were charged with simple assault, disorderly conduct, harassment, and criminal conspiracy. Police are thankful that the fire-in-the-hole idiots, mostly high school students, often videotape their exploits and put them up on YouTube, making it easier to apprehend them. In one case, an employee at a Taco Bell took matters into her own hands. When she found the video of two teens hitting her with a

32-ounce drink, she befriended one of the boys on MySpace, got his address, and called his mother. Both boys in that case were charged with assault and were ordered to do one hundred hours of community service, pay for cleaning up the mess at the restaurant, and post an apology on YouTube. Whatever happened to the good old days when bored kids in cars spent their evenings bashing in mailboxes with baseball bats?

Inflation'll Do That to a Guy

A man in San Antonio, Texas, upset when he found out his Taco Bell Beefy Crunch Burrito was $1.49 instead of 99¢, took out a BB gun and shot at the manager through the drive-thru window. No one inside the restaurant was hurt, but the shooter stayed in the parking lot waving a couple of guns around, and then he got all serious when the police arrived and he started shooting at them. He proceeded to run off and barricade himself inside a nearby motel room. Police finally arrested him after throwing tear gas into the room. The burrito-starved man faces three counts of attempted capital murder.

The McBeatdown

A twenty-one-year-old McDonald's manager was caught on tape beating up one of his employees. Video shows the manager putting the seventeen-year-old employee in a headlock and then punching him in the face. The beatdown was over a misunderstanding about the employee working late.

THE ONES YOU LOVE

I think Miss Piggy said it best after one of her many altercations with Kermit: "You always hurt the one you love." How true! We all have the best of intentions with our wives, husbands, girlfriends, parents, and children, but then we go ahead and get drunk and drive off, leaving our daughter at the gas station.

Ninja Dad

Every boy wants to be able to tell his friends that his dad's a ninja. Right?? Well, one four-year-old boy in Scottdale, Pennsylvania, got that wish . . . sort of. Police arrested the boy's father when the man was found outside at one thirty in the morning, dressed all in black, and "playing ninja on the street." The man told police he was out for a jog; however, police at the scene noticed mud on the man's knees. The man finally admitted he was acting out a fantasy of portraying a ninja "employed for espionage and assassinations." Ninja dad was arrested for endangering the welfare of a child since he had left his young son home alone. When asked why he was playing by himself, the man responded, "There are not a lot of people who want to play ninja."

The Vending Machine Made Me Do It

A thirty-three-year-old man is behind bars after a vending machine "made him" attack his mother, breaking her wrist. Police reported that the man said that "the Pepsi machine at Costco made him hurt his mother."

Mother/Son Outing

The drivers of two speeding vehicles, one chasing the other, were pulled over by Maryville, Tennessee, police early one Sunday morning. The forty-six-year-old chaser was the twenty-four-year-old chasee's mother. Both suspects failed sobriety tests, and the son even managed to fall over backward while taking the test. No word on why mom was chasing her kid.

Brush with the Law

How do you know when it's time to move out? How about you're twenty-six years old and your mom still cleans up after you, albeit not with your best interests in mind? Well, one mom was cited with harassment after she told her son that she used his toothbrush (the one he was still using to brush his teeth) to clean the bathroom. The bathroom hadn't been cleaned in months, and mom was just a tad fed up, it seems.

Mommy Issues

A twenty-eight-year-old Memphis, Tennessee, man was arrested after stealing his mother's prescription Xanax from her bra while she was sleeping. She kept the pills near her person so her son couldn't get to them. That didn't stop him, so she called the cops on him. They found the man hiding under a neighbor's SUV.

Frozen Mis-steak

In February 2011, a woman in Houma, Louisiana, was charged with aggravated battery against her boyfriend after trying to put her drink in the freezer. Realizing the freezer was too full, she got upset, blamed her boyfriend for the lack of space, and smacked him in the face with a frozen beefsteak. The boyfriend called the authorities and the girlfriend was arrested at the scene.

The Glue That Binds

During the summer of 2009, a lover's quadrangle in the small town of Stockbridge, Wisconsin, got ugly when four women (the wife, two girlfriends, and a friend who hadn't slept with the man) decided to seek revenge on the philandering guy. Did they slash his tires? Confront him? Tell him to take a hike? Not quite. One of the girlfriends lured him to a motel and tied him up. Instead of giving him the promised rubdown, however, she texted the other women. Once they arrived, they proceeded to beat the man and superglue his penis to his stomach. Then they ran for it. The man was able to escape by chewing through his bindings. He was treated at a local medical facility and released, but was shortly thereafter arrested on charges of child abuse, theft, unlawful phone use, and harassment. Three of the women were charged with participating in false imprisonment, sexual assault, and misdemeanor battery.

Left Speechless

A fifty-seven-year-old woman in Sheboygan, Wisconsin, was arrested for biting off her seventy-nine-year-old husband's tongue and grabbing his genitals while he gave her a good-night kiss. (Granted, she was on the toilet when he went in for the smooch.) She then ran outside and started singing Christmas carols while her husband called 9-1-1. The dispatcher had no idea what the man was saying, but sent a unit over to the home. When police arrived, the wife blew a party horn in one of the officer's ears and threw a cup of coffee at them. Doctors were able to reattach the man's tongue, and although he didn't wish to press charges, his wife was arrested and admitted to a psychiatric hospital for some much-needed testing.

A Deadly Proposal

They were in love, and it was supposed to be a moment they'd remember forever. And though neither is likely to forget what happened, it's not exactly a story either will recall fondly. A Los Angeles, California, man decided to pop the question to his longtime girlfriend at a local Burger Stop. He even wrote "Will You Marry Me?" on the back window of his car . . . the very car he then used in his attempt to run over his girlfriend after she refused him. After driving his car over the sidewalk and through some bushes, he narrowly missed his now-ex in the Burger Stop parking lot. The rejected man ran away on foot. Police helicopters spotted him a short time later, still carrying the flowers he had planned to give his bride to be. He was caught and charged with felony assault with a deadly weapon.

Daughter Dearest

A seventeen-year-old honor student is facing aggravated assault with a deadly weapon charges after pistol-whipping her mother and forcing her, at gunpoint, to drive to a car dealership and buy her a car. Knowing that the gun was in her daughter's purse, the mom bought the girl a Nissan 305Z. Only after finding the gun while the girl was at school did she notify authorities. The teen is in juvenile detention, and even though the mother didn't wish to press charges (the daughter had been accepted to "several Ivy League schools"), authorities are moving ahead, especially since A) the gun was stolen property and B) the mom also found drugs in the girl's room.

Double the Crazy

Forty-nine-year-old twins from Houston, Texas, are in jail facing felony murder charges after police found the men's eighty-nine-year-old mother's decomposing body in the entryway of their home. The two men had spent three months living alongside the dead body. What's worse, they admitted that their mother had fallen while they were watching a football game and since she didn't ask for help, they left her there. She eventually died three days later. Three days in which the men continued to live in the house, providing no water or food or help of any kind. One of the twins said they left her there because they couldn't afford to pay for medical treatment and "didn't have the money to bury her." Police found bank statements at the scene showing balances of nearly $700,000.

Hood Ornament

You know how the story goes: Husband and wife have a fight late at night. Husband is probably high. He runs out of the house, gets behind the wheel of the family minivan, and decides to take off. "Oh, no, you don't," says the wife, chasing after the minivan as it begins to drive away. She follows the van for a second or two, shaking her fist while the husband speeds away. That's not, however, how the story ended in Manteca, California. In this case, the wife jumps on the hood of the minivan. The husband keeps driving while the wife holds on to the windshield. He takes her on a thirty-five-mile trip, reaching speeds of one hundred miles per hour. He finally stops. She rolls off and is helped by a witness who followed the van for most of its journey. The wife is taken to the hospital and treated for hypothermia (it was near freezing that night). Meanwhile, the husband returns home where he is arrested and later charged with attempted murder, kidnapping, and domestic assault.

"Mom, I'm Starving!"

A man from Samara, Russia, who was arguing with his mother decided to win the argument by hitting her over the head with a brick and then strangling her to death with an electric cable. He then threw himself a two-day party, spending all his mother's pension money on vodka and gambling machines. After returning home penniless, with his mother's body frozen out on the balcony, the man quickly ran out of food. Facing starvation, he decided to start eating his mother, who was perfectly preserved out there in the bitter cold. He made some mommy soup, pasta with mommy meat sauce, and more mommy morsels over the next month. After he was arrested, the man confessed and said, "I did not like the meat very much. It was too fatty. But I was so hungry, I had to eat it." Incredibly, the judge in the case reduced the man's fifteen-year jail sentence by nine months because the judge believed he only ate his mother because he was starving.

Not Parents of the Year

Most parents like to think they're doing good things for their children. The following parents can't possibly think that. In fact, they may be in a secret competition to see who can mess up their kids the quickest. My money's on story number one.

➔ A Florida couple is facing child endangerment charges because they apparently left their two infant children (fifteen months and nineteen months—not sure how they pulled *that* off!) in the car while they got drunk in a bar. Police were called to the scene after someone working in the bar noticed the couple taking turns going back and forth to the car, where the witness heard babies crying. (Note: If I gave birth to two kids four months apart, I'd want to be drunk, too!)

➔ A Gilbert, Arizona, woman was confronted by police in a Target parking lot after receiving calls from witnesses who heard the woman threatening to kill her three-month-old baby. The forty-three-year-old woman screamed "I will kill you!" several times at the crying baby. She admitted to officers that she threatened the kid, and then she handed the baby to one of the cops and said, "Give this baby to [Child Protective Services]; I can't do this." That's just what they did.

➔ A mom arrived at school for a talk with the principal about a fight her eleven-year-old daughter was involved in. But when the woman saw that her daughter had lost the fight, she approached the victor and demanded a rematch. When her daughter began losing the second fight, mom jumped into the action and slapped the other girl on the back of the neck a few times. "She kept accusing me of stuff. She put her two hands in my face and was like, 'Why did you jump on my daughter the other day?'" said the other little girl. Mom faces battery charges and two counts of child abuse. She is also no longer able to have contact with her daughter.

➔ German police are investigating a couple after they offered their baby for sale on eBay. The ad said, "Baby—collection only. Offer my nearly new baby for sale because it cries too much. Male, 70 cm long." The opening bid was 1 euro. The mother said it was a joke; however, she has to undergo psychiatric testing.

➜ A stranger knocks on your door one Saturday night and asks if you can watch her eighteen-month-old son for fifteen minutes because she is having car problems. You agree and she leaves, but never returns. This scenario took place in Palmetto, Florida. The man who agreed to watch the child called authorities after six hours, and although they were able to identify who the mother was, they didn't find her until she returned two days later to the home where she dropped the kid off. She was arrested and it's believed she was using drugs.

Heil Daddy

When forty-one-year-old Matthew Roberts set out to find out who his biological father was, he was nervous and excited. Imagine how he felt, however, when he found out that his dad was Charles Manson, mastermind of the 1969 murders of nine people, including the pregnant actress Sharon Tate. Father and son are in communication with each other, with dad signing each of his letters with a swastika. Ah, those precious moments with loved ones . . .

In Service of Mother

A forty-eight-year-old mom was arrested in Smyrna, Georgia, after her eleven-year-old son called the cops on her. The woman had apparently thrown cans of beer at her children and then beat her fourteen-year-old son for refusing to roll her marijuana joints for her. The younger son also had scratches from where mommy dearest had thrown a knife at him.

Car Wash Discipline

Police were searching for two women caught on surveillance video at a car wash restraining a screaming two-and-a-half-year-old girl, then using a high-pressure hose to blast her with water. "It looks like the girl probably had an accident—urinated or spilled a drink," police said. The car pulled out of the car wash after the torture without washing the car, leading authorities to speculate that the women drove to the car wash and paid the $2 for the express purpose of meting out punishment. The girl's mother turned herself in to authorities once the video went viral on YouTube.

Drunk Driving: A Family Affair

Police stopped to assist a truck that was stuck in the mud in Flint, Michigan, only to find that a thirteen-year-old boy was behind the wheel. The boy's forty-one-year-old father, who was in the passenger seat, explained politely that he was too drunk to drive, so he let his son take the wheel. Too bad the kid was drunk, too. Police reported that the boy "even said he didn't want to drive because he was too drunk." Dad was arrested for child endangerment, allowing an intoxicated person to drive his vehicle, and allowing an unlicensed minor to drive. Meanwhile, the boy was sent to juvie court, where he faces DUI charges.

Cinderella Had It Easy

A couple is facing felony child cruelty charges after forcing one of their children to live outside in the backyard. Police, responding to a 9-1-1 hang-up call, witnessed a man and women yelling in front of three young girls. While two of the girls looked normal, the oldest was dirty and "ill-clothed." It seems the eleven-year-old girl spent most of her time in the yard doing manual labor and wearing dirty clothing, and she could only come inside at night, when she slept on the floor with no pillow or blankets. All this while her two stepsisters played and lived inside. The girl wasn't allowed to use the bathroom and had to bathe outdoors and wash her clothing in a bucket.

Now, Where Did I Put Her?

A woman in New Castle, Delaware, was recently arrested for drunk driving and reckless abandonment. The charges stem from an incident at a gas station. The drunk woman took her four-year-old daughter to a portable bathroom outside the station. Then she finished filling up, paid for the gas, and drove away, leaving her daughter in the bathroom. A truck driver found the girl alone outside the bathroom and called authorities. Meanwhile, state troopers were busy responding to a call that came in about a disabled vehicle and some drunk woman going on about not being able to find her daughter.

No Time Like the Holidays

There's nothing we humans love to do more than celebrate the holidays. However, there's something about that three-day weekend that brings out the inner criminal in us. Now, don't get me wrong: crime never takes a holiday. But the wrongdoing done on and around all the major holidays is particularly bizarre. So whether you're looking forward to a festive occasion or just excited about taking a couple days off from work, beware the Halloween pranks gone wrong and bad Santas.

Comet Does Cupid

A forty-six-year-old Cobb County, Georgia, man was arrested on December 20 for leading a group of middle-school football players on a neighborhood vandalizing spree. The man drove the kids around in his pickup truck and had them rearrange people's holiday reindeer lawn ornaments. *Huh, what's so horrible about that?* you might be asking yourself. Well, according to the warrant, the man's mission was to find "reindeer lawn ornaments and place them in sexually suggestive positions." He was charged with several misdemeanors including contributing to the delinquency of a minor.

Bad Santas

Santa is supposed to be all about "ho, ho, ho," gifts under the tree, and sugarplums dancing in heads. So why is it that he's always getting into so much trouble? Maybe it's because he's only employed one day a year . . .

➔ Santa was pulled over in Germany for speeding. He said he was in a rush because he still had "packages to deliver." Santa had his license taken away.

➜ In what could have only been a confusing sight for young children, forty drunk Santas, protesting the fact that Christmas was becoming too commercial, ran through Auckland, New Zealand, robbing stores and assaulting people.

➜ Two Santas were arrested at a mall in Dayton, Ohio. They were part of a larger crowd of up to one hundred Santas who arrived at the mall to sing off-color Christmas carols. One of the two detained Santas was arrested for striking a police officer.

➜ A "Santacam" was installed in a shopping center in South Wales to allay parents' fears after several high-profile pedophile cases in Britain . . . just in case.

➜ Santa was arrested in North Platte, Nebraska, for possessing pornographic images of children.

➜ Santa, while visiting a farmer's market in Houston, Texas, was arrested and charged with sexually assaulting a teenage girl.

➜ Santa was arrested in Parma, Ohio, for attempting to kidnap a twelve-year-old girl as she walked to school. In his sack, police found a box of candy canes and a unicycle.

➜ Christmas shoppers in Germany were horrified to find statuettes of Santa in shop windows seemingly giving the Nazi salute. Even though the toy Santas look like they're simply pointing skyward, they were quickly removed, as it is illegal for anyone (or anything, apparently) to perform the stiff-armed salute in Germany.

➜ In Sparta, Washington, Santa was arrested after trespassing in a family's yard and hugging the children who were playing there. He drunkenly asked the children if they knew where his reindeer were. One of the kids, a nine-year-old girl, said, "I knew it wasn't the real Santa because Santa doesn't drink alcohol."

➜ Santa was arrested in December 2009 for throwing glass balls filled with paint at the famous Welcome to Fabulous Las Vegas, Nevada sign. He was wearing his Santa hat, shorts, and a cardboard barrel.

➜ The BBC reported that a handcuffed Santa, being led away by police for fighting, caused children watching a Christmas parade in Great Yarmouth to cry. "Children dissolved into tears as they watched the red-cloaked imposter trade blows with a teenager in the market place," the article reported. Officers then invited the crying children to the police station where they could see for themselves that the bad Santa was in fact a fraud. A spokesperson for the department said, "Norfolk Police are certain that the real Santa would not approve of people behaving in this way and of course he will continue his pre-Christmas visits and delivery of gifts everywhere on Christmas Day." Whew!

IN OTHER NEWS: A forty-five-year-old man dressed as an elf in order to have his picture taken with Santa at a Georgia mall was arrested after he told Santa he had dynamite in his bag. Meanwhile, a nineteen-year-old woman was arrested in Indianapolis, Indiana, for ripping off Santa's beard outside Conseco Fieldhouse before an Indiana Pacer's game. Ouch!

Girl Gets Her Wish

In 2008, a Pharr, Texas, man was arrested after a nine-year-old girl sent her Christmas wish to Santa Claus and asked for a relative to stop touching her and her sister. She got her wish, and the man faces ninety-nine years in jail.

This Costume Blows

A Nebraska teenager who dressed up as a mobile Breathalyzer for a Halloween party was—can you guess?—pulled over on his way home and arrested for drunk driving. (Yes, he was given a Breathalyzer test.) And he wasn't the first. An Ohio college student was pulled over the previous Halloween wearing a similar costume. He was just as drunk as the Nebraska teen.

Big Baby

A forty-seven-year-old man was arrested on Halloween for disorderly conduct. At the time, he was wearing a full baby costume that included bib, bonnet, and diaper. Witnesses say he was cursing at children and adults while demanding candy. The big baby whined that homeowners called the police only because he was trick-or-treating and they thought he was too old to receive candy. He admitted that even though he had been drinking, he wasn't drunk.

Prank Dead on Arrival

Two women got in a bit of trouble with California police after pulling a Halloween stunt that had half the California Highway Patrol as well as U.S. Marine military police and homicide detectives racing to the scene of the "crime." The women decided to see what would happen if they wrapped a mannequin in a bloody sheet and dumped it on an on-ramp to Interstate 40. Deputies found the two women on a nearby hill watching with binoculars as every emergency worker in the county converged on the scene. The women were arrested and charged with suspicion of causing a false report of an emergency.

IN OTHER NEWS: Two children in Galatia, Illinois, walked into their home on Halloween and saw what looked like a dead body in their living room. The six- and eight-year-olds ran to a neighbor's house and called 9-1-1. By the time the cops arrived, the parents of the kids had straightened everything out and said it was just a practical joke they were playing on their kids. Nice parents . . .

Gang-Related Vacation Tours

For your next vacation, consider Los Angeles, California, where you can now take a high-end bus tour of historic and current gang crime scenes and hot spots. Highlights of the tour include:

➔ the Los Angeles County Jail: unofficial home to more than one hundred and twenty thousand gang members.

➜ the Los Angeles River riverbed: where they filmed the *Grease* drag race scene and home to "some of Los Angeles's most prolific tagging crews."

➜ the Symbionese Liberation Army Shootout: the location of one of the largest gun battles in American history—more than ten thousand bullets fired!

➜ the birthplace of the Black Panther Party.

➜ Florence Avenue: the official street of the LA riots.

➜ the birthplace of Raymond Washington's East Side Crips, where you can meet reformed members of the gang who have dedicated their lives to ending gang violence.

LA Gang Tours was founded by Alfred Lomas, who used to be a gang member but is now a minister. His website states that the mission of the tour is "to provide an unforgettable historical experience for our customers . . . with a true firsthand encounter of the history and origin of high-profile gang areas." The tours are led by guides from the South Central area who have hands-on knowledge of the inner city lifestyle. Tickets are $65.

Although this may sound like a wacky way to exploit his neighborhood, some of Mr. Lomas's objectives are to create jobs, to raise money for economic development, and to educate people about gang life and solutions for it. He has even helped negotiate a cease-fire between the gangs so children can get to school safely and the tour buses can travel through without problems.

IN OTHER NEWS: Looking for something unique for you and your loved one to do on Valentine's Day? Well, you can visit the National Museum of Crime & Punishment in Washington, DC, and experience "Crimes of Passion." This special romantic exhibit starts off with each loving couple being handcuffed together by on-staff "wardens." They are then led on a tour of the museum with special displays explaining various crimes of passion, including the "Valentine's Vampire." And great news! You get to keep the handcuffs!

JUDGES, COPS, PREACHERS, AND OTHER CROOKS

Here's a whole bunch of stories about crimes committed by the people who are supposed to be the good guys, the ones upholding the law, the bastions of our community. Unfortunately, just because someone has a badge or a collar or a Bible in their belt doesn't make them any better than the rest of us. In fact, sometimes it makes them worse.

Preacher Acting Badly

The pastor of the Shining Light Baptist Church in Clay County, Alabama, was shot and killed after attacking police officers with a brush axe. The officers were there to serve the man with a warrant and a protection order. He chopped off one of the officer's hands, which was later successfully reattached. This came a week after the pastor was Tasered when he threatened officers with a high-powered rifle. A friend of the pastor's lamented, "He was a good Christian man. I have no idea, no clue . . . I never knew him to be violent."

Thou Shalt Not Embezzle

Catholic nuns seek to imitate the life of Christ. As such, they take vows of obedience, chastity, and poverty. Nowhere in those vows is there room for stealing buckets of money for your gambling addiction. Yet that's just what one Catholic nun was accused of when she was charged with stealing nearly $1 million from Iona College in New Rochelle, New York. As the college's vice president of finance, she allegedly stole around $80,000 a year for ten years before she was relieved of her duties and shipped to a convent in Pennsylvania. She used her college credit card for personal expenditures and turned in fake invoices and bills for the money she stole. One colleague at the school mentioned she spent a lot of time in Atlantic City.

Ratings War

Wallace Souza was a Brazilian state politician and television personality who starred in *Canal Livre*, the Brazilian version of *Cops*. In the wildly popular crime program, murders of criminal figures were detailed and even filmed. In fact, Souza had the uncanny luck of often arriving at the scene of murders before the police did. This "luck" made the cops suspicious, especially when, during one live show, a reporter walked through a forest to record a burning corpse. How did the reporter know the body was even there? Well, it seems Souza hired hit men to carry out the murders in order to boost the show's ratings. He was accused of contracting at least five murders as well as drug trafficking. The police intelligence chief in charge of the investigation said, "The order to execute always came from [Souza]

and his son, who then alerted the TV crews to get to the scene."
Souza got his ratings boost, and since some of the victims were drug
trafficking rivals of Souza's, getting rid of them also helped out his
drug business. Totally win-win right? Souza was arrested along with
his son, the show's producer, and dozens of others. He was charged
with being part of a criminal organization, forming an armed gang,
drug trafficking, and illegal weapons. He died in prison before he
could stand trial.

The Craigslist Cop

A woman in Mansfield, Texas, woke up one morning to find two people
loading her family's portable basketball goal into their truck. She ran
outside to confront them, but they said there was an ad on Craigslist
offering the goal as well as the woman's tetherball pole for free to the
first people to pick them up. The woman had never even heard of the
classified advertising website, but sure enough, Craigslist had this ad
listed under her address: "Free basket ball goal and tether ball pole. At
dead end of roadway beside my home . . . don't knock its placed out
there for you to come get. will delete when gone. thanks." It turns out
that the family's neighbor, a police officer, didn't like having to look at
them all the time. Police aren't quite sure what to charge the man with.

The Rubdown

Orange County, California, prosecutors have charged a forty-seven-
year-old former police officer with felony burglary and misdemeanor
counts of impersonating a peace officer after he was caught pretend-

ing to be a massage parlor inspector and demanding free rubdowns and cash from masseuses. One January day, the impostor walked into the Golden Spa massage parlor with a badge and said he was following up on a complaint. He then complained of back pain, and a masseuse gave him a back rub. Then he complained of front pain, but that rubdown was refused and the masseuse got suspicious and called 9-1-1.

Self Investigation

A police officer in Stockholm, Sweden, reported to his superiors that he had no leads in the bank robbery he was investigating. The man was by no means upset over his failure, since he was the one who robbed the bank to begin with. An hour after robbing a significant sum from the bank at gunpoint, he returned as the lead investigator. The officer was only caught a month later when fellow officers became suspicious after he bought a new car with cash . . . using bills from the heist.

Pump It Up

An Oklahoma judge was sentenced to one year in prison. His crime? Well, it had something to do with what went on behind the bench. Witnesses testified to at first hearing a sh-sh sound in the courtroom whenever this particular judge was presiding. Then a court reporter recounted when she first discovered the source of the sound: Through a small gap between a drawer and a door she saw the judge with his pants undone using a penis pump (supposedly created to enlarge the penis or combat erectile dysfunction). A star witness also saw the judge pee in a trash can behind the bench and shave his scrotum—all while court was in session. The judge denied ever using the device, saying it was a gag gift from a friend. However, jurors handed in a guilty verdict after hearing a tape in which the whooshing sound could be clearly heard over the sound of a witness giving testimony in a murder trial.

Judge Jumpy

A Waukesha, Washington, county circuit judge was charged with disorderly conduct after jumping on the hood of her ex-boyfriend's car, kicking the car, and screaming. At the time, the car was parked in front of another woman's home and the man was inside with the other woman.

Beach Patrol

A Marin County, California, sheriff's deputy was relieved of duty for using his patrol car's dashboard camera to film scantily clad women at the beach.

Child Psycho-iatrist

A forty-seven-year-old child psychiatrist was arrested at a beach after she attempted to kidnap two children. Witnesses state they saw the woman approach three children while they were playing in the water. She then grabbed two of them and screamed, "These are my kids Mattie and Meredith!" The father of the two children was able to free his children, but not without a minor struggle.

Bowling on Duty

Eleven members of a Florida antidrug task force were caught on video playing Wii Bowling at a home they had just stormed in order to execute a search warrant. The cops had no idea that the house had a video surveillance system, which snared them playing the game "enthusiastically," according to news reports. The video was broadcast by a Tampa television station, and all the officers involved had to receive hours of "retraining" (whatever that means).

Choking on the Paperwork

Two police officers in the Russian city of Ulyanovsk picked up a drunk man in their cruiser, but since it was the end of the day, they decided to let the man out near some old garages instead of taking him back to the station to fill out the paperwork. The drunk man began complaining about how he was being treated, so the now-enraged policemen hit and strangled the man to death.

Cruel Confessions

A retired Catholic archbishop in the United States, who once paid $450,000 to a man who accused him of date rape, claimed in his memoir that, "We all considered sexual abuse of minors as a moral evil, but had no understanding of its criminal nature." He also wrote that he had accepted "the common view that it was not necessary to worry about the effects on the youngsters: either they would not remember or they would 'grow out of it.'" Needless to say, those who suffered abuse at the hands of clergy members were furious.

The Juvie Judges

Imagine you're a high school student with a grudge against your vice principal. You decide to spoof him on MySpace, but you get caught. What's the worst that could happen? A slap on the wrist? An apology and perhaps some counseling? Well, if you ended up in Judge Mark Ciavarella's courtroom in White Haven, Pennsylvania, this would have gotten you three months at a private juvenile wilderness camp.

The unfortunate young woman who received this punishment was just one of hundreds of children who were sent to juvenile lockups run by two private companies. The connection between these cases were two Wilkes-Barre judges, Ciavarella and Michael Conahan, who in 2009 were charged with taking millions of dollars in payoffs from the two juvenile detention centers for sending kids their way. The scam included sending kids to prison for minor offenses such as not bringing lawyers with them. Other offenses included stealing loose change from cars and writing prank notes in school. An attorney for the Juvenile Law Center said, "I've never encountered, and I don't think that we will in our lifetimes, a case where literally thousands of kids' lives were just tossed aside in order for a couple of judges to make some money." In 2011, Ciavarella was convicted of twelve charges including racketeering, money laundering, and conspiracy, and he could face more than ten years in jail. More than four thousand of his cases were dismissed by the Pennsylvania Supreme Court. Conahan's case has yet to go to trial.

Tax Seasonal Disorder

Charles J. O'Byrne was a top aide to New York's Governor David Paterson until he resigned in 2008. O'Byrne stepped down because he didn't file tax returns for five years and owed more than $300,000. His lawyers explained during a press conference that O'Byrne couldn't file his taxes because he suffered from a medical condition known as "late-filers syndrome." The American Psychiatric Association assured the *New York Times* that there was no such thing.

I Really Wanna Hold Your Hand

A sergeant in the Miami-Dade County, Florida, police department was arrested for domestic violence and aggravated assault with a deadly weapon after assaulting his girlfriend for not holding his hand at a Miami Heat basketball game. First, he forced her to take a cab home alone after the game. When she got home, he was waiting for her with his service pistol in hand. He forced her to pack her bags while he aimed the gun at her. He also dragged her by her hair and then pulled out the big gun: an AR-15 assault rifle. The officer has been relieved of duty.

CELEBRITY CRIMES

You can shake a tree and at least two celebrity criminals will fall out. They're everywhere, doing all sorts of mean and nasty things. There are the drugs, the shoplifting, the domestic violence, the awful excuses, and, in most cases, the getting away with it because ultimately everybody wants their autographs.

He Belongs in a Cage

In April 2011, actor Nicolas Cage was arrested for domestic abuse in New Orleans. His Saturday evening was a special one. First he visited a tattoo parlor, demanded a tattoo, and began throwing his clothes around. He then asked employees of the shop to call police because "he didn't remember where he lived." Afterward, he argued with his wife over the correct address of their rental house. He grabbed her roughly by the arm to pull her to where he thought they were staying. Then, according to reports, he started hitting parked cars. The cops were called and Cage began yelling at them and daring them to arrest him. They did. (The best part of the story is that he was later bailed out by reality-TV star Dog the Bounty Hunter. Of course.)

Weirdo's Blood in His Veins

Charlie Sheen's life of crime began at a young age, when he was busted for possession of marijuana at the tender age of sixteen. The judge, a friend of the family, dismissed the charges. At seventeen (or, some reports say, fifteen), Sheen and some friends used credit card receipts fished out of the trash at the Beverly Hills Hotel to go on a four-day shopping spree. They bought televisions, jewelry, expensive watches, and more. His punishment? His mom paid for the merchandise.

Let's now move to the Charlie Sheen Rap Sheet Timeline:

1990: Sheen "accidentally" shot his fiancée, Kelly Preston, in the arm. Here's how he summed up what happened: "That was a complete accident. I wasn't even in the room. She picked up a pair of my pants, to get them off the bathroom scale so she could weigh herself one morning. A little revolver fell out of my back pocket, hit the bathroom floor, and went off. It shot a hole through the toilet and she got hit in the leg with shrapnel . . . But she was fine. She got two stitches and I had to get a new toilet." Punishment: no legal repercussions, but the engagement was called off.

1995: After being born again, Sheen married the model Donna Peele. Soon after, Sheen admitted to being a client of Heidi Fleiss, the infamous Hollywood madam. He revealed that he spent around $50,000 for Fleiss's call girls. Sheen was also sued by a college student who claimed he hit her in the head when she refused him sex. The assault case was settled out of court. Peele divorced Sheen within eight months.

1997: Sheen pleaded no contest to battery charges brought by ex-girlfriend Brittany Ashland, who claimed he threw her to the floor. Punishment: one year suspended sentence, two year's probation, and a $2,800 fine.

1998: Sheen suffered a massive overdose after trying to inject cocaine. Punishment: rehab.

2006: His wife, Denise Richards, filed a restraining order, saying he pushed her and threatened to kill her. Punishment: ugly divorce, but no jail time.

2009: Sheen was arrested on felony menacing charges after allegedly threatening his wife, Brooke Mueller, with a knife while in a drunken rage. Punishment: one night in jail, thirty days in rehab, thirty days of probation, and thirty-six hours of anger management counseling. Hanes, the underwear company known for its undershirts that are often called wife-beaters, finally dropped Sheen as one of their pitchmen.

2010: Police were called to the Plaza Hotel in New York where a drugged-up and naked Sheen had trashed a hotel room and allegedly locked a naked porn star in the bathroom. He caused around $7,000 in damages. Punishment: avoided jail, even though he was in violation of his probation; received a raise for his role on *Two and a Half Men*, becoming the highest paid star on television.

IN OTHER NEWS: Charlie Sheen's father has been arrested a whopping sixty-six times. However, Martin Sheen has been arrested during civil disobedience protests, not for trashing hotel rooms.

The Celebrity Crime Quiz

Test your knowledge of celebrity rap sheets with this fun, yet strangely sad, quiz!

1. Which Baldwin brother has been arrested?
   A. Alec
   B. Daniel
   C. William
   D. Stephen

ANSWER: B. Although Alec once punched a photographer who then tried to put him under citizen's arrest, it's his brother Daniel (Detective Beau Felton in *Homicide: Life on the Street*) who has a lovely set of mug shots to show mother. In 2006, Daniel was arrested for stealing a GMC Yukon. He was also charged with possession at that time. He had been arrested previously for drugs in 1998 when he was found running naked through the halls of New York's Plaza Hotel screaming, "Baldwin!"

2. Which of the Beatles have records—criminal, not platinum?

ANSWER: Only Ringo doesn't have a criminal record. Paul, George, and John have all been arrested at one point or another for possession of marijuana.

3. Which rapper has never been arrested?

   A. Snoop Dogg
   B. Dr. Dre
   C. Eminem
   D. Jay-Z
   E. Kanye West

ANSWER: None of the above. I searched high and low but couldn't find a rapper who had never been arrested. (I mean, I could have put Will Smith in there—his record's clean—but calling him a rapper is the same as calling hard lemonade booze.)

Snoop Dogg was convicted of felony narcotics possession in 1990, charged with illegal firearms in 1993, and acquitted of murder in 1996. He also has a few possession charges to his credit. In 2006, Snoop was banned from British Airways after he started a brawl at Heathrow Airport in London in which several police officers were injured.

Dr. Dre was sentenced to house arrest after breaking the jaw of a record producer. He pleaded no contest to a 1991 assault charge in which he attacked the host of the show *Pump It Up*, picking her up by her hair and ear and smashing her face and kicking her in the ribs. The civil lawsuit was settled quietly.

In the early 2000s, Eminem was charged with two felonies: carrying a concealed weapon without a license and assault with a deadly weapon. He received probation and community service.

Jay-Z pleaded guilty to a misdemeanor charge that resulted in three years of probation for the 1999 stabbing of a record executive at a nightclub.

Kanye West was arrested in 2008 after getting into a fight with a photographer outside of a nightclub in England. He was released with "no further action." Charges were dropped. West was also charged with felony vandalism after taking on two cameramen at Los Angeles International Airport and messing up their cameras. Charges were dropped.

4. Match the celebrity with his or her crime:

Heather Locklear	Urinating on the Alamo
Johnny Cash	DUI and a separate hit-and-run incident
Naomi Campbell	DUI while driving a golf cart
Ozzy Osbourne	Assault with a deadly mobile phone
Bill Murray	Picking flowers on private property

ANSWERS:

Heather Locklear: DUI and a separate hit-and-run incident. Locklear was arrested in 2008 for driving under the influence of a controlled substance. She pleaded guilty to a lesser offense. In 2010, she was arrested for a hit-and-run incident in Westlake Village, California, in which she hit and injured a no-parking sign.

Johnny Cash: The man who sang "Folsom Prison Blues" was arrested for picking flowers on private property. Johnny Cash never served any prison time, no matter what his songs say; however, he had several run-ins with the law, including a narcotics arrest in 1965 (back when that was a big deal). He was also arrested for trespassing while picking those flowers.

Naomi Campbell: Assault with a deadly mobile phone. Campbell has been arrested for assault a few times, with her most famous being the 2006 arrest for assaulting her housekeeper with a jewel-encrusted mobile phone. The housekeeper ended up requiring several stitches, and Campbell was charged with second-degree assault. She pleaded guilty to reckless assault and was sentenced to five days community service.

Ozzie Osbourne: Urinating on the Alamo. In 1982, Osbourne was arrested in San Antonio, Texas, for lifting up his dress (not sure why he was wearing a dress) and urinating on the Alamo.

Bill Murray: DUI while driving a golf cart. Only Bill Murray could find a way to get arrested while drinking and driving a golf cart. The incident occurred in 2007 in Stockholm, Sweden, and the famous actor was stopped by police late one night while driving along a public road, attempting to return to his hotel in a golf cart. The police smelled alcohol on Murray's breath, and the rest, as they say, is history.

5. Which crime has Robert Downey, Jr., not been arrested for?
    A. Drunk driving
    B. Possession of drugs
    C. Violating parole
    D. Starring in *Johnny Be Good* (1988)

ANSWER: D. Good thing actors can't be arrested for horrible movies.

6. *Diff'rent Strokes* ("What'chu talkin' 'bout, Willis?!") was a popular sitcom that ran from 1978 until 1986. It was the heartwarming story of two orphaned kids from Harlem who are adopted by a rich man

and his daughter. The show made stars out of the three child actors, but as with most child actors, trouble followed them, leading many to proclaim a *Diff'rent Strokes* curse. Can you match the *Diff'rent Strokes* child star with his or her crime?

Arnold (Gary Coleman)   Attempted murder

Kimberly (Dana Plato)   Robbery and forging prescriptions

Willis (Todd Bridges)   Assault

ANSWERS:

Arnold: Assault. In 1998, Gary Coleman was charged with assault after he punched a woman while at a shopping mall. She had asked for his autograph, and when he refused the request, she started making fun of him. Coleman was also involved in an altercation with a photographer in a parking lot. Coleman allegedly argued with the man before getting in his car and backing up into him. Coleman died in 2010.

Kimberly: Robbery and forging prescriptions. In 1991, Plato held up a video store in Las Vegas, Nevada, with a pellet gun. The clerk called 9-1-1 and said, "I've just been robbed by the girl who played Kimberly on *Diff'rent Strokes*." She was arrested fifteen minutes later when, for some unknown reason, she returned to the store. She was arrested again in 1992 for forging a prescription for Valium. She stayed out of trouble after that, but she died of an overdose in 1999.

Willis: Attempted murder. Bridges has battled cocaine addiction since the 1980s, and in 1988 he was arrested and charged with the attempted murder of a drug dealer. He was acquitted. In 1993, he was once again arrested for attempted murder. This time he stabbed a man with a kitchen knife during an argument. He was acquitted after it was determined that the man had been in the process of attacking Bridges with a sword. Bridges has since cleaned up his act and seems free and clear of the *Diff'rent Strokes* curse.

Celebrity Excuses

The only thing more fascinating to the jaded American public than watching a celebrity get caught breaking the law is listening to the lame excuses they come up with.

THE CELEBRITY: Winona Ryder

THE CRIME: Shoplifting

THE EXCUSE: After getting caught leaving a Saks Fifth Avenue in Beverly Hills with thousands of dollars worth of merchandise in her purse, Ryder said she simply forgot to pay for the stuff. Reports also surfaced that she told the security guard, "I was told that I should shoplift. The director said I should try it out." Ryder was convicted of grand theft and given three year's probation.

THE CELEBRITY: Nicole Richie

THE CRIME: DUI

THE EXCUSE: After the 2006 arrest for driving the wrong way on a highway while high, Richie explained to the officers that she only took the Vicodin because of bad menstrual cramps.

THE CELEBRITY: Paris Hilton

THE CRIME: Cocaine possession

THE EXCUSE: Oh, that little baggy of cocaine that just fell out of my purse? I thought it was gum.

THE CELEBRITY: Shelley Morrison (*Will & Grace*)

THE CRIME: Shoplifting

THE EXCUSE: When Morrison was arrested for attempting to steal more than $400 worth of goods from a department store, she simply said, "I don't know why I did it. I remember buying the shoes and I remember walking outside and having three security people starting to yell at me to take off my jacket. They were taking these tacky things out of my jacket. It was stuff I wouldn't have bought and it was on sale and when they tallied it up, it came to $98, but for some reason the store's policy was they were going to charge me full price. I've since seen therapists and they explained to me that I left no room for myself and sometimes the mind has a mini earthquake."

THE CELEBRITY: Lindsay Lohan

THE CRIME: Cocaine possession

THE EXCUSE: After cocaine was found in Lohan's pockets in 2007, she exclaimed, "These aren't my pants." (Then, after being sentenced to probation and counseling, she missed a court appearance in 2010, allegedly because she lost her passport and couldn't get back to the United States. She also missed an alcohol counseling session because, according to her lawyer, her uncle died. When asked if Lohan attended the funeral, her lawyer had to admit she hadn't. Finally, when she was forced to wear an alcohol-monitoring ankle bracelet, Lohan's lawyer asked for it to be removed because she had to film reshoots for a movie. A spokesperson for the studio, however, told CNN that the film was in the can and no reshoots were scheduled. Have to give this celebrity an A for effort . . . lots and lots of effort!)

THE CELEBRITY: Eddie Murphy

THE CRIME: Soliciting prostitution

THE EXCUSE: After being pulled over by Los Angeles, California, police in 1997 with a transvestite prostitute in his car, Murphy went into lame PR mode. "I was being a good Samaritan. It's not the first hooker I've helped out. I've seen hookers on corners . . . and I'll pull over . . . and they'll go, 'Oh, you're Eddie Murphy, oh my God,' and I'll empty my wallet out to help."

THE CELEBRITY: Tatum O'Neal

THE CRIME: Attempting to buy crack

THE EXCUSE: She didn't know it was crack and the death of her dog drove her to do it.

THE CELEBRITY: Idaho senator Larry Craig

THE CRIME: Lewd conduct

THE EXCUSE: After being arrested in 2007 outside the men's room at the Minneapolis-St. Paul International Airport for attempting to solicit sex from an undercover cop, Craig said that he just had a naturally "wide stance" and was only trying to pick up some paper off the floor.

THE CELEBRITY: Tennis pro Richard Gasquet

THE CRIME: Cocaine use

THE EXCUSE: When Gasquet tested positive for cocaine, leading to his suspension by the International Tennis Federation, he claimed the cocaine got in his system after French-kissing a woman in a nightclub.

THE CELEBRITY: Charles Barkley

THE CRIME: Passing a stop sign and drunk driving

THE EXCUSE: He was in a rush to meet up with a prostitute.

THE CELEBRITY: Dina Lohan (mother of Lindsay Lohan)

THE CRIME: Stealing a Carvel ice cream cake

THE EXCUSE: The store wouldn't honor her daughter Ali's "free ice cream for life" card (it was non-transferable). Police helicopters were brought in to the scene.

IN OTHER NEWS: Here's a normal person using a celebrity as an excuse for her bad behavior: An Ohio woman who was arrested for lighting a bar's bathroom on fire stated that she did it because she "felt stressed because of the death of Michael Jackson."

The Whizzinator

Actor Tom Sizemore's problems with drugs led him to jail time, domestic abuse charges, and poverty. Happily, the actor cleaned up his act on *Celebrity Rehab with Dr. Drew*, and his career is rebounding. However, during the bad years, Sizemore inadvertently helped publicize a bizarre product created to help defeat drug tests. Called the Whizzinator, this kit came with dried urine, heater packs, instruction manual, and a false penis (available in several skin tones, including white, tan, Latino, brown, and black). Simply add water to the dried urine, place it in the Whizzinator, activate a heater pack, and hide it in your underwear. When it's time to provide a urine sample, whip out your Whizzinator and deliver the goods. In 2005, Sizemore was caught using the device when authorities found out the pee wasn't warm enough to have come from his body. The ruse got him sent to jail.

Meanwhile, in 2008, federal prosecutors won a multi-count indictment against the device's maker, Puck Technology, for fraud and selling drug paraphernalia. The devise was taken off the market, but don't fret! You can own one now for the low, low price of $139.95, as long as you don't mind having a strap-on wet sex simulator with synthetic urine show up on your credit card bill. (The device was simply renamed and reclassified as a sex toy.)

Foxy's Beauty Regime

Rapper Foxy Brown was arrested in 2007 for using a beauty supply store's products in their bathroom. When the store tried to close for the day, Foxy refused to leave, yelling, "I have to finish my hair!" When reminded that she really needed to pay for the merchandise ("This is not a beauty salon, it's a store!"), Foxy sprayed weave glue at an employee and spat at her. She then tried to hit the cops who arrived to arrest her.

THE iDioT METER

We all do silly or dumb things every now and then. Most of the time, however, we're lucky enough to keep it out of the news. The people you're about to meet are not as lucky or as smart as the rest of us. Each has been rated, for your convenience, according to their stupidity level, with 1 being more unlucky than completely idiotic and 10 being the most moronic morons on the planet. Feel free to assign your own numbers, as these ratings are completely subjective.

Just Sign Here

One man learned a valuable lesson after getting arrested at his home for robbing a Walgreens: Don't tell the person you're robbing your name. A twenty-nine-year-old man entered a Walgreens with a weapon and demanded drugs. The pharmacist asked the robber for his name and birth date so he could look up his prescription. The man gave his real name and then the pharmacist told the man he couldn't fill his prescription for another month and to come back then. The confused criminal was captured at his home the next morning.

IDIOT METER: 7 (I mean, really! He went in thinking he was robbing the place and left thinking he had just tried to fill a prescription.)

Ash Holes

Up to five teens thought they hit the jackpot when they broke into a home and discovered a large amount of drugs, which they stole and began snorting immediately. Too bad they were snorting the cremated remains of two Great Danes and dear old dad. What makes their cluelessness even more spectacular was that the remains were in urns. Perhaps one could understand their behavior if the ashes were in plastic bags, but alas, no. Once they discovered their mistake, they threw the remains in a lake.

IDIOT METER: 10 (Mostly since the "drugs" were in urns.)

Bragging Gets You Nowhere

A man from Chicago, Illinois, called a local radio station during its popular confessions show to brag about a bank heist he and his friends had committed. The man admitted to tying up employees and stealing around $80,000, which he and his cohorts spent at stores on Chicago's ritzy Michigan Avenue. An employee of the bank that was robbed was listening to the radio program and called police. They traced the bank robber's call and made the arrest. At the time, authorities had no other leads since no one at the scene of the crime could provide good descriptions of the crooks. The captured suspect told the FBI that he called the station to win a prize and has denied any involvement in the crime.

IDIOT METER: 9 (Nothing like snatching defeat from the jaws of victory.)

Hike!

A nineteen-year-old man attending a concert by Further (featuring members of the Grateful Dead) at the University of Pittsburgh crashed through a window. He reportedly got down in a football stance, yelled "Hike!" and charged through the window. The man died before he could be questioned, and toxicology reports were pending as of this writing.

IDIOT METER: 4 (The secondhand smoke at the concert was probably enough to give the man a serious contact high and make any of his decisions questionable.)

Sliced Chicken

A Tulare County, California, man died after receiving several cuts to the leg from a rooster that had knives attached to its legs. An anonymous tip led police to a field where a cockfight was supposedly going on. In the chaos that ensued, the man was stabbed by the bird, and doctors were unable to control the bleeding.

IDIOT METER: 6 (The only thing you should ever put on a chicken is seasoning.)

A Not-So-Bright Idea

Two men (one twenty and the other sixteen) wielding machetes and knives attempted to rob a sports club in Sydney, Australia, ignoring the fifty motorcycles in the parking lot. Evidently there was a meeting of the Southern Cross Cruiser Motorcycle Club that evening. The leader of the bikers told CNN, "These guys were absolutely dumb as bricks. I can't believe they saw all the bikes parked up front and they were so stupid that they walked past [them]." The robbers walked

into the bar that was next to the room where the bikers were meeting and yelled at the patrons to drop to the floor as they emptied the cash registers. The bikers, hearing the commotion, grabbed anything within reach not bolted to the ground and rushed the two young men with chairs, tables, and more. One of the would-be crooks crashed through a plate-glass door and then jumped off a balcony to escape. He was apprehended by police shortly thereafter and hospitalized. The second man was caught by the bikers and beaten; they "hogtied him with electrical wire and left him for the cops."

IDIOT METER: 9 (Come on, already! Fifty motorcycles!)

IN OTHER NEWS: A Berlin man was caught stealing items from jackets in a coatroom at the annual Christmas party for officers of the police criminal investigations unit. He was confronted by thirty-five officers. "He was definitely surprised," said a police spokesperson.

Calling for a Date

A Washington County, Oregon, sheriff's deputy was investigating a noise complaint. A woman answered the door and assured the deputy that she would indeed turn down the music. The deputy left, but then the woman called 9-1-1. Let's hear her emergency: "A police officer left my house just now . . . He's the cutest cop I've seen in a long time. I just want to know his name. Heck, it doesn't come very often a good man comes to your doorstep." The incredulous dispatcher asked, "You need him to come back there?" "Oh, I'd like that, yeah," the woman responded. When asked for a reason, she said, "Blame it on my dog." The dispatcher, still confused, asked again what the problem was. The woman leveled with the dispatcher: "Honey, I'm just going to be honest with you, okay? I just thought he was cute. I'm forty-five-years-old and I'd like to meet him again, but I don't know how to go about doing that without calling 9-1-1. I know this is not absolutely in any way, shape, or form an emergency, but if you would give the officer my phone number and ask him to come back, would you mind?" The same deputy returned to the woman's house and promptly arrested her for misusing the 9-1-1 system, which is punishable with up to a year in jail.

IDIOT METER: 3 (Hey, he was cute and she was lonely. What's wrong with that? Oh, yeah—she called 9-1-1 for a boy's phone number.)

Game Over

A twenty-three-year-old man in Clemson, South Carolina, was struck by an SUV while jaywalking across a four-lane highway . . . except it wasn't really jaywalking. He was playing a real-life version of the video game Frogger, where the player controls a frog that has to jump across several lanes of traffic and make it safely to the other side. He and a few friends had been discussing the popular 1980s video game, and he decided to give a demonstration. At "Go!" the man ran across the highway, moving back and forth between lanes before being hit by a Lexus, whose driver won't face any charges. As for Frogger man, police suspect alcohol may have been involved. "I've never heard of anything like this," said the chief of police.

IDIOT METER: 10 (What would have happened if they were talking about Space Invaders?)

Call Kindergarten Cop

Two women in Victorville, California, were charged with interfering with the "peaceful conduct at a school" when an argument they were having turned physical, leading to a brawl . . . at their children's kindergarten graduation ceremony. Several people ended up fighting, and although nobody was seriously hurt, school officials had to place the school on lockdown until police arrived.

IDIOT METER: 8 (Kindergarten graduation brawl? Seriously? What could they possibly have been fighting over? Whose kid could eat glue better?)

Hoping to Hit It Big

A New York bookkeeper stole more than $2 million from her employer, Great South Bay Surgical Associates, and used the loot to buy lottery tickets, hoping to hit the jackpot. She spent around $6,000 a day on lottery tickets. It's not clear if she ever won. She pleaded guilty to grand larceny and faces some serious jail time.

IDIOT METER: 9 (Um . . . why didn't you just steal the money and buy drugs or something? You'd get a better return on your investment.)

Remote Possibilities

A French thief who had just made off with a television and some hunting rifles was arrested when he returned to the scene of the crime for the television's remote control.

IDIOT METER: 7 (Now, criminals, repeat after me: *Don't* return to the scene of the crime. *Don't* return to the scene of the crime.)

Joyrides

A drunk man outside a Wisconsin ski area stole an ambulance with the paramedics and patient still inside. The twenty-four-year-old man drove the ambulance around the parking lot for a while before being apprehended. Meanwhile, a man in Chicago also stole an ambulance, but this time the paramedics and a family member of the man were inside. He drove for about three blocks before being stopped by a roadblock set up by local firefighters. "He probably thought he was helping," said Fire Media Affairs Director Larry Langford.

IDIOT METER: 2 (Who hasn't wanted to go for a joyride in an emergency vehicle?!)

You Coulda' Knocked

A woman in Deerfield, Illinois, heard strange noises coming from outside her apartment complex. She assumed it was landscapers working in the yard. However, upon closer inspection, it was actually a neighbor of hers breaking into her apartment by cutting through her door with a twenty-inch chain saw. The woman escaped by jumping off her second-floor balcony, and the man was later arrested and charged with trespassing and criminal damage to property.

IDIOT METER: 6 (Yes, chain saws are cool; however, you may wish to rethink your "breaking in" method next time. Choose something that doesn't draw quite so much attention to yourself.)

Shopping Spree

When the wallet of a Columbus, Ohio, man proved to be empty of cash, the two men who ambushed him outside his home decided that the man and his girlfriend would take them shopping with the debit and credit cards they did find. The couple was forced to withdraw cash at an ATM and then told to hit the local Walmart. The girlfriend was sent into the store to buy two Sony PlayStations while the crooks stayed in the car and held the man hostage. The woman later told a local TV station, "(Walmart was) out of PlayStations. So my next thing was, 'I really would like to speak to somebody—a security officer.'" The crooks made the man drive off before police could arrive, leading authorities on a wild, high-speed chase that only ended when the man drove the car into a dead end. One of the crooks, thinking quickly yet not intelligently, threw his gun onto the man's lap, saying, "Tell the cops it's your gun." The man, no longer being held at gunpoint, did no such thing, and the two eighteen-year-olds were arrested and charged with multiple crimes.

IDIOT METER: These kids start off at a 5, hit 7 by the time they send the girlfriend into Walmart, and reach a whopping 10 when they give the gun to the hostage.

Thieves Tracked by Loot

Three Long Island, New York, thieves were caught by their stolen goods. Thinking they had stolen fourteen cell phones, the threesome was dismayed to learn that they had instead stolen GPS devices. Police simply tracked the devices and arrested all involved.

IDIOT METER: 4 (It was an honest mistake. All those gadgets look alike.)

Plane Stupid

A business executive on a Delta Air Lines flight en route to Boston from Dallas needed something the flight attendants just couldn't supply, so he took matters into his own hands, literally. The fifty-five-year-old man placed a blanket over himself and the young woman sleeping next to him. He then unfastened her seatbelt, unbuttoned her pants, and assaulted her. The woman woke up immediately, ran to the back of the plane, and reported the man. The man was sentenced to seven years in jail.

IDIOT METER: 11 (This guy broke the meter with his stupidity.)

Train Stupid

Thieves in Austria made off with a thirty-pound safe but couldn't open it. One of the crooks came up with the bright idea of placing it on a railroad track and waiting for a speeding passenger train to open it for them. A train did indeed collide with the safe, sending around $6,000 flying everywhere and nearly derailing the train, which sustained extensive damage. The thieves, meanwhile, fled empty-handed. According to a spokesperson for the national railway, this was the first time a train had ever been used to open a safe in the history of the country.

IDIOT METER: 8 (Not sure what the thieves thought would happen, but hey, they did manage to get the safe open.)

Breakup Stickup

A Colorado man, angry over being dumped by his girlfriend, decided to seek vengeance by robbing the bank where she worked. A Colorado Springs police sergeant reported, "He robbed a bank where people knew him. Everybody was like, 'Oh, that's Gary.'" Police caught up to the crook at a homeless shelter, where the man tried to run with the loot stuffed in his sock. He ran right into two officers. One officer told newspapers, "I've been doing this for twenty-four years, and I've caught a lot of bad guys, but not that easily. It doesn't really get any easier than that."

IDIOT METER: 9 (In the man's defense, at least his ex-girlfriend was at lunch during the holdup.)

IN OTHER NEWS: A Columbus, Ohio, man returned to the scene of the crime (a home he had robbed two hours earlier) to ask one of his victims out on a date. The woman recognized the man, had a relative call the cops, and the man was arrested in front of the home.

Deaf and Dumb

A forty-one-year-old man was arrested for attempting to rob a bank in Berlin, Germany. He burst into the bank and yelled, "Hand over the money!" When a teller asked if he wanted a bag, the robber responded, "Damn right it's a real gun!" The bank manager, realizing the man was deaf, set off the alarm, which was "ridiculously loud." Police arrived and arrested the deaf man.

IDIOT METER: 1 (Especially since the criminal then sued the bank for exploiting his disability.)

Tag, You're an Idiot

In 2007, a man accused of leaving a restaurant in El Lago, Texas, without paying was seen heading toward a vacant building. When the police arrived, they entered the building to search for him. One officer, "trying to inject some humor into the situation," called out, "Marco!" The chew-and-screw diner, whose name was not Marco, was located after he responded, "Polo."

IDIOT METER: 2 (Hey, give the guy a break. It's a fun game.)

Facebooked

A Washington, DC, family went home one December day to find their home burglarized. They had lost several items, including one of the children's laptops. The crook then did something really stupid. He posted a photo of himself wearing the boy's new coat on the boy's Facebook page. Police are now using the photo to find the crook.

IDIOT METER: 5 (Some days it is difficult to find something interesting to post on Facebook.)

IN OTHER NEWS: A man is behind bars for stealing two diamond rings and other items from a home. While in the home, he decided to check his Facebook page on the homeowner's computer. Then he forgot to log himself out.

EXCUSES, EXCUSES

In 1981, a Texas man mistakes his mother-in-law for a large raccoon and hacks her to death. Now, there are several possibilities here: 1. The man, even after committing murder, could still tell a good mother-in-law joke. 2. The man was loony. 3. Thinking quickly (but not well), he came up with the best excuse he could while under intense scrutiny. Then he stuck with his story. This chapter is not so much about the crime as the excuses the accused often use to get out of their predicaments. Heck, even science has gotten into the action, providing a classic excuse defense lawyers can add to their arsenal: Bad guys are uglier than good guys and hence have low self-esteem.

The Decimal Point Defense

When a $1,772.50 deposit showed up in a Bloomsburg, Pennsylvania, couple's bank account as $177,250, the husband and wife team did what any normal Americans would do: They withdrew the money, quit their jobs, bought a new car, and moved to Florida. When the law finally caught up to them and charged them with felony theft, they claimed it was all just a big misunderstanding. You see, they often got large checks because the husband is a roofer, so they didn't pay attention to exactly where that decimal point was. They simply weren't aware of any banking error. Except . . . the husband only earned about $4,000 the previous year installing roofs. The couple spent more than $120,000 before they were caught.

The Bucket List Bandit

A fifty-one-year-old woman who was arrested for robbing a Bank of America claimed she did the deed because she wanted to cross it off her bucket list, which is a list of things to do before you die. (The term was popularized by the 2007 movie of the same name.) There is no evidence that the woman was ill or dying, and she will be spending the next five years of her life in prison after pleading no contest to the charges. (Jail time, I believe, was not on her list.)

Some Ugly Statistics

A 2005 paper in the *Review of Economics and Statistics* found that unattractive people committed more crimes than average-looking people. Beautiful folks committed the fewest crimes of all (not including celebrities—see page 61). The paper, entitled "Ugly Criminals," states that attractive people are more successful in their careers and earn more, which puts ugly people at a disadvantage. They earn less, have fewer friends, and are therefore more likely to turn to a life of crime. The study has already been called "a handy profiling tool" by the BBC.

Best Hide-and-Seek Player Ever!

A man in North East, Maryland, was caught trying to rob a local BP convenience store when the owner opened up the store in the morning and found a pair of feet dangling from the ventilation system in the ceiling. After police freed the man and arrested him, the suspect said that they had it all wrong. He had simply been playing hide-and-seek with other adults who stopped looking for him when they couldn't figure out where he was.

Conversion Math

A California woman was pulled over in Essex County, Ontario, for driving 140 kilometers per hour in an 80 km/h zone. The woman explained that her Mercedes-Benz's speedometer only had miles per hour and she didn't know how to convert miles to kilometers. She was fined nonetheless.

Tag Team

A mother/daughter tandem were arrested for choking and threatening an elderly Walmart greeter in Elyria, Ohio. The forty-nine-year-old mom yelled racial slurs at the seventy-one-year-old man, pushed a shopping cart into him, and grabbed his throat. Meanwhile, the pregnant twenty-one-year-old daughter threatened to blow up the store and told the greeter he was dead meat once her boyfriend found out about the incident. And what exactly was "the incident"? The greeter had asked the women to show him a receipt as they left the store, which is standard operating procedure at most Walmarts.

Big Excuse

There is truly no excuse for child molestation, but that didn't stop one New Hampshire man from giving it a shot. The fifty-seven-year-old man told investigators that he had been sexually assaulted as a child by Bigfoot. One detective replied, "I've had a few that have claimed abuse, but never by a mythical creature."

Kitty Porn

A forty-eight-year-old man was arrested for possessing child pornography on his computer. In fact, police found more than a thousand images. The man, however, claimed that his cat must have walked on the keyboard and inadvertently downloaded the images. The cat would jump on the keyboard when he left the room and "strange things" would then appear on the computer.

The Beanie Defense

A California woman was sentenced to six months in prison in 1998 for stealing credit card numbers and charging $8,000 to other people's credit cards. Her excuse? She was addicted to Beanie Babies, those little stuffed animals that were all the rage back in the late nineties. She used credit card numbers stolen from the hotel where her husband worked to purchase more than two hundred of the toys, until police raided her home and confiscated them. "It was like a drug," the woman stated. "Once I started, I couldn't stop. It was like being addicted." Along with the jail time, the woman was forbidden to have any contact with Beanie Babies for five years, and she had to pay back all the money she stole.

Baby Brand

A Georgia man pleaded guilty to tattooing the letters *DB* on his three-year-old stepson's shoulder blade. The man admitted that he tattooed his kid, but said that he didn't remember doing it because he was drunk. (Like that makes it any less frightening!) The mother attempted to hide the tattoo by applying temporary tattoos over the real one, but she wasn't charged with anything. When asked what the letters stood for, the demented tattoo artist said, "Daddy's Boy." Meanwhile, incredibly, the judge who heard the case admitted, "I am trying to figure out why this is illegal. Is it illegal to pierce your little girl's ears?" She finally fined the dad $300, put him on probation, and forbade him from having any contact with his daddy's boy.

WHY THEY ATTACK

Sometimes the crime isn't as interesting as the motive. For instance, a stabbing is a stabbing—sure, it can go down in a number of different ways, but at the end of the day, it's pretty much the same thing every time: someone with a knife plunges it into someone else. Case closed. The only real suspense is whether the stabber gets stabbed back or if the stabbed person makes it to the hospital before bleeding out. However, sometimes the motive for a criminal attack simply needs to be shared due to its incredibleness. So, without further ado, here are a few vignettes of people attacking other people, for the LAMEST REASONS EVER. I mean, we've got smelly feet, dog poop on the lawn, Elmo, snowballs, and even who got to use the microwave first. Enjoy the show.

Shootout at the Dog Poop Corral

Although each man's story differs as to who shot whom first, the cause of this Mississippi shootout was one man's dog pooping on the other man's lawn. The dog owner accused the lawn owner of trying to shoot his dog a week earlier and challenged the lawn owner to a duel, saying, "Just meet me at the levee and I'll shoot you down."

The lawn owner accused the dog owner of shooting first and received several shotgun pellet wounds to the hands, shoulder, chest, and side for all his efforts, but was not seriously wounded. The dog owner ended up with assault charges, and police are considering charges against the lawn owner as well.

IN OTHER NEWS: A Chicago man shot and killed a neighbor who let his dog pee on his perfectly manicured lawn. The shooter was convicted of second-degree murder but only sentenced to four years of probation.

Movie Mayhem

You might want to think twice before telling a fellow moviegoer to turn off their cell phone. A California man trying to see *Shutter Island* with some friends asked a woman to stop talking on her cell phone. Seems reasonable, right? Another woman seated nearby even said the man was polite about it. However, the chatty woman's companion left the theater in a rage and returned with a five-inch-long thermometer and stabbed the man in the throat. The man lived, and his assailant faces life in prison. The deputy district attorney told the *Los Angeles Times*, "We've all had enough of this blatant disregard for decency: You can't go to a movie theater without worrying about saying the wrong thing to the wrong person and being stuck with a thermometer in your neck." The attacker was also found guilty of possessing a firearm. So even though he had a gun, he decided to use a thermometer? Perhaps he didn't want to make too much noise. It was a pretty good movie, after all.

Wrenching Crime

A thirty-one-year-old man, perhaps upset over not having been invited to his pregnant sister's wedding, showed up at the reception and hit her in the mouth with a large wrench. He also pushed the groom's mother to the ground and fought with the groom. He was charged with assault with a weapon and disorderly conduct.

You're in Elmo's World Now

A man hired to wear an Elmo suit for a children's event was attacked by a man who later said he felt threatened by the *Sesame Street* star. He began throwing punches at Elmo, but Elmo fought back and broke a couple of the attacker's fingers. (Thankfully no children were present.) A police lieutenant reported, "[Elmo] just wandered into the Guitar Center to look at instruments." Police also said in a statement that the suspect was taken to the hospital "where he would receive treatment for his injuries and undergo a mental evaluation." Elmo was unhurt.

Shootin' Mad

An Arizona man was arrested for shooting at Hualapai Valley firefighters. He had reported a tree fire, but when the fire crew arrived there was no fire: The man wanted them to get his cat out of a tree. The firefighters refused. The incensed man ran to his home and came back outside with a small revolver. No one was injured, but the man was charged with multiple felony aggravated assault with a deadly weapon counts.

The Case of the Smelly Feet

While hanging out and drinking with friends, an eighteen-year-old woman was challenged to do a backflip. She took off her shoes and one of her friends, a nineteen-year-old man, started teasing her that her feet smelled. Police found the man a short while later with a steak knife embedded three inches into his back, and the woman was charged with second-degree assault with a deadly weapon. One of the man's lungs collapsed, but he recovered. Meanwhile, the woman was sentenced to fifteen months behind bars and must write a paper "exploring how drinking alcohol to excess can destroy lives." The judge in the case said, "Let me be absolutely clear: This case is not about smelly feet. It is about binge drinking."

Did She Learn That Move from Tyson?

A woman at a party in Lincoln, Nebraska, took offense at being called fat by one of the partygoers as he walked out the door. She chased him down the block, tackled him, and bit off his ear.

Sore Loser

A twenty-five-year-old man drove his pickup truck across a lawn, over a mailbox, and toward several people. He then drew a rifle and held it against the forehead of the man who—wait for it—beat him at arm wrestling. The suspect went into a rage after the loss, and ended up charged with four counts of aggravated assault with a vehicle and one count of aggravated assault with a deadly weapon.

Snowball-istics

Why did one Massachusetts man beat up the other? Well, both men are facing charges of assault and disorderly conduct after one of the men threw a snowball at the other man's car. The car owner stopped, got out of the car, and beat up the snowball thrower.

Family Values on Display

A fifty-three-year-old woman was arrested in Washington, DC, in 2011 for attacking Paul Gauguin's painting "Two Tahitian Women" at the National Gallery. The painting depicts two women, one topless and the other exposing one breast. The attacker tried to pull the painting off the wall while yelling, "This is evil!" And when that failed, she banged on the painting's Plexiglas protective covering. The woman told police, "I feel that Gauguin is evil. He has nudity and is bad for the children. He has two women in the painting and it's very homosexual. I was trying to remove it. I think it should be burned. I am from the American CIA and I have a radio in my head. I am going to kill you." The suspect was sent for a "mental observation hearing."

Heated Argument

A Walgreens employee was arrested for stabbing a colleague with a large kitchen knife. They were fighting over who got to use the microwave in the employee break room first. A sheriff's office spokesperson said, "They didn't get along to begin with. Who could use the microwave first became a major issue."

Pee-nut

A Nebraska man was arrested for throwing detergent bottles full of pee into people's backyards. The man told police it was a longtime hobby of his.

Coffee Caper

A man from Chicago, Illinois, upset at his employers at a metal-finishing plant where he worked, placed urine, lead acetate, and other substances in the office coffeemaker over a period of several months. After multiple employees reported vomiting after drinking the coffee, a hidden camera was installed that caught the man spiking it. Why was he angry enough to cause the sickness and possible deaths of his fellow coworkers? His superiors forbade him from drinking coffee in a certain area of the factory.

Tough Crowd

A twenty-five-year-old woman was attacked by six other women at a sports bar in Stamford, Connecticut, in October 2009. The woman was knocked to the floor, punched, kicked, and had her hair pulled. She suffered bruises and a chipped tooth, and all six of the women were arrested on assault charges. Why the rough treatment? The woman was singing karaoke ("A Dios le Pido" by Colombian pop idol Juanes) and the others didn't like her performance. A police press release stated that the six women "made derogatory comments about the other female's singing ability (or lack thereof)."

Really Tough Crowd

The *New York Times* reported in February 2010 that karaoke singing often leads to violence in the Philippines, especially if the singer is belting out Frank Sinatra's version of "My Way." One karaoke singer said, "I use to like 'My Way,' but after all the trouble, I stopped singing it. It can get you killed." The article goes on to report that authorities don't know why this particular song causes so much violence, but theories range from a low tolerance for bad singing to the "arrogant" and "triumphalist" lyrics. Up to six people have been killed so far over this particular song in the past decade, and police have their own subset category for these murders, calling them "The 'My Way' Killings." The violence has prompted bar owners across the country to remove the song from their karaoke playlists.

IN OTHER NEWS: In Thailand, a man killed several neighbors in an uncontrollable rage after they sang John Denver's "Take Me Home, Country Roads." Who can blame him?

School Bus-ted

A Bridgeport, Connecticut, woman forced her way onto a school bus and began beating on and perhaps spitting on two twelve-year-old girls. Some witnesses say she threw the first punch, while others state someone hit her from behind. Either way, the twenty-nine-year-old woman found herself in an all-out brawl, with one child needing medical attention. The reason for the attack was that one or more of the students were throwing trash out of the bus windows and some of it hit the woman's car. The woman was charged with criminal trespass, breach of peace, third-degree assault, and risk of injury to a minor.

Shootin' Mad

A thirty-two-year-old man was arrested after shooting a sixteen-year-old girl in the knee. Police told a local news reporter that the man argued with the girl and then shot her because she refused to give him a cigarette, as it was her last one.

NAKED AND STUPID

All the stories in this section deal with people who are doing stupid and illegal things while wearing very little or no clothing. Actually, I'm going to go out on a limb and say that just about anyone hanging around in public with almost no clothing on is about to do something stupid (aside from the *already* stupid thing of taking one's clothes off publicly). And if the (other) stupid action hasn't happened yet, wait for a minute or two. It will.

Explosive Excuse

A forty-two-year-old man was arrested in a Walmart parking lot for standing up naked in the bed of his truck and shaking himself at two women walking past. The man explained to police that it was all due to his "explosive diarrhea"; he was using his underwear to clean himself off. But investigators found no evidence of any bowel movements on said underwear, and the man was arrested and charged with indecent exposure.

Mail Call

A postal carrier in Wisconsin was arrested for delivering mail in the nude. He claimed that he only wanted to cheer up one of his customers who seemed "stressed out." He had told the woman he would deliver the mail naked in order to make her laugh. She dared him, and he did. After his arrest, he admitted that it was a stupid thing to do.

Here Comes the Bride

A thirty-three-year-old Maryland woman was sentenced to five years in jail for breaking into her neighbor's house wearing a bridal skirt and veil . . . and nothing else. The woman used her head to break a dining room window, and the shattered glass caused the homeowner to cut an artery in his arm. The bride-to-be testified at her trial that a combination of pot and cold medicine led her to believe that she was getting married but that her mother was locked in the neighbor's basement. She was convicted of second-degree assault, burglary, and reckless endangerment.

The Naked Truth

A Picayune, Mississippi, man was arrested after being found naked in a cemetery. Yes, he had an explanation: He was trying to take pictures of spirits and skin is the best way to show spirits' orbs of energy. The forty-seven-year-old man had only intended to take his shirt off, but apparently got carried away. Incredibly, he was charged with indecent exposure anyway.

Indecent Exposures

A forty-year-old West Bend, Wisconsin, man was arrested and charged with eight counts of lewd and lascivious behavior and five counts of disorderly conduct after placing photographs of his privates on the windshields of women's parked cars. He told police that he thought the women "would find it funny."

Stripped for Cash

When billionaire shipping tycoon Alki David wanted publicity for his new website, he didn't take out an ad. Instead he offered to pay $1 million to the first person who streaked in front of President Obama during a speech with the business's domain name across his (or her) chest. In order to qualify for the money, the streaker also had to yell "battlecam.com" six times within earshot of the president. A Staten Island, New York, man did what David asked at the president's speech in Philadelphia in October 2010. He was promptly arrested on disorderly conduct and indecent exposure charges. And not only that, but David initially refused to pay the streaker because he hadn't met all the demands. He never paid the full amount even though traffic to his website doubled after the stunt.

IN OTHER NEWS: The streaker wasn't the only publicity hound at that particular speech. A man was briefly detained by the Secret Service after throwing a book at the president. The man wanted to publicize the book, but the title of the book was never released.

I'll Have a Sexpresso to Go

Forget Starbucks! The Seattle/Tacoma area of Washington State is awash in bikini barista espresso stands, with one website listing more than one hundred locations. The premise of a bikini barista stand is simple: Buying coffee is good, but buying coffee from a scantily clad female is even better (at least if you belong to the half of the population that's into that sort of thing). With shops like Hot

Chick a Latte, Java Juggs, Bare Espresso, Lace 'n' Lattes, and Sweet Cheeks, it's a wonder some of these shops haven't gone a little too far and provided more than just sugar and a shake with your java. Well, that's exactly what happened at the local Grab 'n' Go Espresso in Everett, Washington. Five baristas were arrested and charged with prostitution for charging customers to touch their breasts and buttocks. They also were paid up to $80 to strip while preparing their orders. Detectives, during a two-month investigation (hmm . . . why did it take them so long, I wonder?), witnessed the women licking whipped cream off one another and posing naked for pictures. One popular game at the store was "basketball," where customers got to throw balled-up money at the baristas, who would then catch the "balls" in their bikini bottoms. The five women were not taken into custody, and since no sex took place on the premises, they faced only misdemeanor charges. The Grab 'n' Go was allowed to remain open.

HiGH CRiMES

People do stupid things when they're drunk, stoned, and/or high or when they want to *get* drunk, stoned, and/or high. They'll wield axes, smuggle drugs in dirty diapers, bark at police dogs, and even report themselves to police for driving while intoxicated. I guess there's only one rule to live by when you're looking to score or have already scored: The only thing worse than a hangover is a hangover behind bars.

Look Mom, One Eye!

A fifty-six-year-old woman was pulled over (after a short chase) near Östernärke, Sweden, for swerving across several lanes on the highway and otherwise driving erratically. A Breathalyzer revealed the woman's blood alcohol was nearly ten times the legal limit. The woman argued with police that she was fine—especially since she had been careful to keep one eye closed to prevent her from seeing double. Despite her conscientious and clever attempt, she was sent to prison for two months.

A Growing Question

A man in Farmington, Connecticut, was wondering what the legal ramifications of growing one marijuana plant were. So he did what any pothead would do: called 9-1-1 and asked the dispatcher. The dispatcher answered the question and the man thanked him and hung up. Officers arrived at his home shortly after and found marijuana, pots, and seeds.

IN OTHER NEWS: A Fargo, North Dakota, woman called the police station asking where she could buy pot. She persisted, even after the dispatcher told her it was illegal to purchase pot, so the dispatcher finally told her they had some in a locker at the station. The woman was arrested when she showed up with $3 for the drugs.

Snorting Grandma?

After pulling over a car in Wyoming, highway patrol troopers found what looked to be a ziplock bag of cocaine. The men in the car insisted it was really the cremated remains of one of the men's girlfriend's grandmothers. Not believing a word these guys had to say (they also had a small amount of pot and drug paraphernalia, after all), the cops called the girlfriend. Sure enough, the baggie held the cremated remains of the woman's grandmother. When asked why her grandmother's ashes were in the car, she replied that they had been very close and she always kept the ashes nearby.

Pampering with the Evidence

A Pennsylvania woman who got pulled over by a state trooper was asked if it was okay to search her vehicle. At that point, the woman asked the trooper to throw away a dirty diaper in a bag of garbage inside the car. The officer, confused as to why she was being asked to throw the diaper away when the driver could have just as easily performed the task, decided to check inside it. Along with the poop, she found pot.

Another Diaper Dandy

A Boston, Massachusetts, woman was arrested for trying to smuggle more than twelve pounds of cocaine in a bag full of dirty diapers. She said someone at an airport in Mexico offered her money to bring the carry-on bag back to the states and that she had no idea what was in it. The cocaine was discovered when passengers on the plane complained of the odor coming from the bag.

I'd Like to Report a DWI

An Iowa City, Iowa, man called 9-1-1 because he thought he was too drunk to drive. Unfortunately, the man was in the car at the time of the call. Police responded and the man was arrested.

Barking Mad

An Ohio man was arrested for barking at a police dog. The dog's human partner was investigating a car accident when he heard the dog barking uncontrollably from inside the police car. Rushing to the vehicle, the officer found the twenty-five-year-old man barking and hissing at the dog. When arrested, the man said, "The dog started it." He appeared extremely intoxicated.

High and Stupid

After confiscating marijuana from a suspect, a Dearborn, Michigan, police officer kept the pot and made some marijuana-laced brownies with his wife. After a couple of brownies, the officer felt like he was overdosing (which is nearly impossible to do with pot) and called 9-1-1. Here's a partial transcript of the conversation (which can be found in its entirety on YouTube):

OFFICER: I think I'm having an overdose and so is my wife.
DISPATCHER: Overdose of what?
OFFICER: Marijuana. I don't know if they had something in it.
Can you please send rescue?
DISPATCHER: Do you guys have a fever or anything?
OFFICER: No. I'm just . . . I think we're dying.
DISPATCHER: Okay, how much did you guys have?
OFFICER: I don't know. We made brownies. And I think we're dead.
Time is going by really, really, really, really slow.

Dearborn police didn't charge the couple, but the cop was forced to resign.

LOL—Pot Purchase Goes Wrong

A teenager in Helena, Montana, while attempting to purchase pot from a dealer, mistakenly texted this message to the local sheriff instead: "Hey Dawg, do you have a $20 I can buy right now?" The quick-thinking sheriff responded in the affirmative and then quickly sent out a detective to pose as a dealer. When confronted with a detective's badge, one of the boys who showed up at the pick-up spot fainted.

Dude, Who Stole My Pot?

An eighteen-year-old man in Provo, Utah, called the police to report that his home had been robbed. The only thing missing was the quarter pound of pot that he was planning to sell. Police found the pot, called the man in to identify it, and arrested him for stupidity . . . and possession with intent to distribute.

IN OTHER NEWS: A man in Darmstadt, Germany, tried to get his money back for the "bad" marijuana he bought by calling the cops to help him with his dealer. The man was arrested for violating drug possession laws when he brought the marijuana with him to the police station.

The Straight Dope

A deputy in Orange County, Florida, was a bit surprised when a man walked up to his car and asked if he was "straight." The man went on, "Do you know what that means? It means 'Do you want to buy some cocaine?'" The officer was in full uniform and sitting in a marked police cruiser. He told the man that, yes, he would like to buy some cocaine, and then arrested him when he produced a bag containing "several pieces of flat white rock substances."

Not Axing Nicely

A twenty-two-year-old man, apparently upset over his father's hospitalization, started drinking and doing drugs to relieve the pain. Then he attacked his mother and the kitchen with an axe. He smashed the oven, the refrigerator, a bedroom door, and then took a swing at mom, narrowly missing her. Then he demanded she stay in his bedroom and watch movies with him. The mom remained in the room for several hours until her son passed out. Then she called the cops.

BAD SPORTS

Competition doesn't always bring out the best in us. In fact, for every heartwarming story of the thrill of victory against inconceivable odds, there are a dozen stories of overblown egos doing stupid illegal things, cheating for the win, and more. Sure, we all want our team's troubled star player to cast aside his or her demons and stay out of jail long enough to provide the winning touchdown, home run, goal, dunk, etc., just as we want our kid's peewee team to beat its crosstown rival. It just seems that people competing against one another provides a petri dish for the germs of bizarre crime to thrive.

No Bull

In 2010, a matador in Mexico City, Mexico, was arrested for breach of contract after running away from the bull he was supposed to be fighting. As the bull charged, the man dropped his cape, ran from the bull, and leapt headfirst over a wall. The twenty-two-year-old torero said, "There are some things you must be aware of about yourself. I didn't have the ability; I didn't have the balls. This is not my thing." The man was released after paying a fine and is considering retirement.

Twin Bill

Jose Canseco, the former Major League Baseball player, one-time Most Valuable Player, and admitted anabolic steroid user, has had an interesting post-baseball life. He's been on a few reality shows, tried his hand at mixed martial arts, and attempted boxing. It's his boxing career that now has him in some hot water. He's being sued by a celebrity boxing promoter for breach of contract after Jose sent his identical twin brother, Ozzie, in his place. Fans in the audience noticed that "Jose's" tattoos were different and notified officials. The promoter quipped, "Maybe I should use his brother and he'll have Jose come instead."

Recruitment Violations

A football coach in San Diego, California, was arrested at Abraham Lincoln High School after a fight with a parent over the recruitment of a player. The coach punched the man in the shoulder and then kicked him in the stomach, causing the parent to fall and hit his head, losing consciousness. What caused the coach to get so angry? Seems he overheard the parent, who was with the other team, trying to recruit one of the coach's best players. By the way, the two teams playing each other were part of a youth league, and the kids were from nine to eleven years old. The coach was arrested on charges of felony battery.

Hero Worship Gone Awry

A man in Oklahoma who received a thirty-year jail sentence for armed robbery wanted his number of years in jail to match his favorite basketball player's jersey number. Boston Celtics star Larry Bird wore number 33, and the district attorney was more than happy to oblige the man, increasing his sentence by three years. The judge in the case said, "He said if he was going to go down, he was going to go down in Larry Bird's jersey. We accommodated his request and he was just as happy as he could be."

Where Are They Now?

It's weird how sometimes sports stars simply disappear from the playing field. One day they're in the box score, and the next they're not. More often than not you don't notice for a while, and then you think, Whatever happened to that guy? Well, here's an update on some past sports stars, with the incarcerated version of Where Are They Now?

→ Rae Carruth played wide receiver for the Carolina Panthers from 1997 to 1999. Where is he now? Carruth was sentenced to nearly twenty years in jail for hiring a hit man to kill his pregnant girlfriend. Carruth helped the hit man by driving in front of his girlfriend's car and stopping while the shooter drove alongside the girlfriend and shot her. She died from her injuries, the baby lived (although he is severely handicapped), and Carruth nearly got the death penalty.

→ Bruno Fernandes de Souza is one of Brazil's best soccer goalkeepers; however, he may have played his last game as he was arrested for masterminding the kidnapping and murder of his porn actress lover. Souza, his wife, and five other people allegedly killed the woman because she had given birth to Souza's baby and wanted to keep it. Reports say the woman was tortured and that her body was fed to some dogs. Souza has stated that he's frustrated because the allegations could hurt his chances of playing for Brazil in the next World Cup.

➜ Ugueth Urbina was a relief pitcher for several Major League Baseball teams, led the league in saves in 1999, and played for the Florida Marlins during their 2003 World Series run. Where is he now? Urbina is serving a fourteen-year sentence in a Venezuelan prison for attacking five employees on his farm with a machete.

➜ Jayson Williams played in the NBA for ten years (1990–1999). Where is he now? Williams is serving five years in prison for aggravated assault after shooting and killing his chauffeur while playing around with a shotgun and then staging the scene to make it look like a suicide.

➜ Plaxico Burress played for the New York Giants team that won the Super Bowl in 2008. Where is he now? Burress was released from jail after serving two years for shooting himself in the right thigh at a New York City nightclub when the illegal Glock he had tucked in his sweatpants slid down his leg and discharged.

➜ Mike Danton played in the National Hockey League from 2000–2004. Where is he now? Danton is serving a seven-year sentence for plotting to kill his agent.

Your Favorite Lineup

If you're a sports fan, take your team's lineup from sometime in the past, be it a favorite year or whenever, and search each of the players on Google to see how many have been arrested. Here's an example of a sports team lineup that would look more comfortable in a police lineup: the 1986 New York Mets. Sure, they won the World Series that year and had one of the most successful and entertaining seasons ever, but most of the team has a criminal record to go along with their record-setting year. Here's a recap:

FIRST BASE: Keith Hernandez got caught up in what was called the Pittsburgh drug trials in 1985. He was called to testify before a grand jury about rampant drug use in Major League Baseball. Hernandez admitted to using cocaine and was one of several players suspended for a full season, although he was allowed to play if he donated 10 percent of that year's salary to a drug-related charity.

SECOND BASE: Wally Backman and Tim Teufel both played second base for the Mets in '86. Both have had trouble with the law. Backman was arrested in 2000 for DWI, and again in 2001 after a fight with his wife, where he pleaded guilty to misdemeanor harassment charges. Teufel was arrested in 1986 along with three other teammates after a fight with off-duty policemen in a bar.

SHORTSTOP: Rafael Santana has no known record.

THIRD BASE: Howard Johnson and Ray Knight platooned at third. They're clean, although Knight was once caught attempting to hunt deer at night and was charged with criminal trespass and "blinding wildlife with lights."

LEFT FIELD: Danny Heep has never broken the law, although he shared duties with Kevin Mitchell, who was a talented and troubled ballplayer with anger issues. He was a gang member in San Diego before becoming a baseball player and was once shot three times. There's also an urban legend that he decapitated his girlfriend's cat during an argument in 1986. His arrest record includes a 1991 arrest on rape charges (which were later dropped), a 1999 felony battery charge for beating up his own father because he hadn't paid his rent, a 2000 arrest for punching another team's manager in the face during a brawl, and a 2010 arrest for attacking someone at a golf course.

CENTER FIELD: Mookie Wilson and Lenny Dykstra shared duties in center field. Mookie's clean; however, Dykstra was arrested for DWI, sexual battery of a seventeen-year-old girl, and grand theft auto. He is currently facing federal fraud charges.

RIGHT FIELD: Darryl Strawberry has had a tough time of things, although he is doing much better these days. His troubled past includes a charge of assault with a deadly weapon after threatening his wife with a semiautomatic handgun in 1990, another assault charge in 1993, failing to file taxes in 1994, charges of willful failure to provide child support and spousal support in 1995, and possession of cocaine and soliciting a prostitute in 1999.

CATCHER: Gary Carter has steered clear of the law, although many say he was the most hated player in the clubhouse.

PITCHERS: Ron Darling, Rick Aguilera, and Bobby Ojeda were also arrested alongside Tim Teufel after the 1986 barroom brawl. Meanwhile, Dwight Gooden was arrested for DWI in 2002, driving with a suspended license in 2003, and punching his wife in 2005. He's served time.

So out of the nine positions on the field, six have records other than statistical. That's a .666 average. Impressive. Can your team beat that?

Put Me in Coach . . . or Else

Cracking the starting lineup is no easy task. It takes talent, aggressiveness, discipline, and sometimes, psycho parents and physical violence.

→ A walk-on backup punter for the University of Northern Colorado, apparently tired of being told to "work harder" whenever he asked how he could break into the starting lineup, took matters into his own hands by stabbing the starting punter in the thigh with a five-inch-long knife. He was convicted of second-degree assault and was sentenced to seven years in prison.

→ A New Jersey dad punched his son's football coach and knocked him out. The incident was over the amount of playing time the dad's kid was receiving. The dad was vice president of football operations of the league, and he was charged with "assault while attending a community-sponsored youth sporting event while juveniles under sixteen were present." The law was created to discourage violence at kids' sporting events.

→ A Philadelphia, Pennsylvania, man pulled a .357 Magnum on his six-year-old son's youth football coach because his son wasn't getting enough playing time. The father was charged with aggravated assault.

Offensive Offensive Lineman

An Oregon State University offensive lineman was kicked off the team after being found drunk and naked in a stranger's home. When police confronted the nineteen-year-old and told him repeatedly to lie on the floor, he instead dropped into a three-point stance, used at the line of scrimmage during games, and lunged at the officers. He was finally tackled by two stun guns.

Do-nut Trespass

Seattle Seahawks rookie wide receiver Golden Tate received a warning from police after a call from Top Pot, a gourmet doughnut shop, saying that they had been robbed of some of their famous maple bar doughnuts. Tate apologized for the incident saying, "Freshly baked. I made the mistake of— A buddy made the mistake [of] going in [and] grabbing a couple. We ate them . . . But, if you ever want maple bars, that's the place to go." Coach Pete Carroll added, "No, I'm not disappointed at a guy being at a doughnut shop at three in the morning when they got maple bars like Top Pot has . . . I do understand the lure of the maple bars."

Game, Set, Murder

We all want to see our children succeed, whether it be in sports, school, or just life in general. We give advice, pay for lessons, and root them on. If, however, you're like one man in France, you'll also drug your children's tennis opponents.

The forty-six-year-old former French army helicopter pilot confessed to spiking twenty-seven of his children's (a son and a daughter) tennis opponents' water bottles with the antianxiety drug Temesta, which causes drowsiness. (It's the drug the father took to calm his own nerves during matches.) The players would complain of feeling sick and dizzy, having weak knees, and nausea. Several fainted and needed medical attention. Things really came to a head when one of the drugged players, who had to pull out of a match against the son, lost control of the car he was driving after falling asleep at the wheel. He crashed into a tree and died. Prosecutors described the father as "an adult who turned his children into objects of his own fantasies of success." They also said to the dad, "Nothing stopped you: players collapsing on the court, the sight of gurneys, of an eleven-year-old girl, a young woman who collapses against a fence." The father, speaking to the parents of the man who died in the car crash, said, "It's something that completely took me over." He's currently serving his eight-year jail sentence. There is no evidence his children ever knew what he was doing. The son gave up the sport, but the daughter still plays and is considered a potential star.

Fans Gone Wild

If you have a hard time understanding the lengths to which athletes will go in order to compete and win, it will upset you even more reading about the shenanigans of the idiots who watch these athletes.

→ Two unidentified Los Angeles Dodgers fans beat a San Francisco Giants fan into a coma, ostensibly because he was wearing a Giants shirt at Dodger Stadium.

➔ A father and son team ran onto the baseball field at Chicago's Comiskey Park and attacked Kansas City's first-base coach Tom Gamboa. He was slammed to the ground and pummeled by the two shirtless attackers. "He got what he deserved," said the thirty-four-year-old dad. The entire Royals dugout jumped on the two attackers, and it was several minutes before order could be restored. "Security did a good job cleaning it up," said one Royals player. "If it wasn't for them, we'd still be beating on those guys."

➔ A stockbroker sitting in the stands as the Chicago Cubs took on the Houston Astros at Wrigley Field in Chicago watched Cubs reliever Randy Myers take the mound. The broker told his brother, who was sitting next to him, "If he throws another home run, I'm going to run out there and give him what for." After Myers gave up a two-run homer soon after his arrival in the game, the crazed fan jumped onto the field and ran at the pitcher. Not realizing Myers was trained in the martial arts, he was felled with one nasty blow from the pitcher.

➔ A light-heavyweight boxing match turned very strange when, just as Tony Wilson was getting pulverized by his opponent, Steve McCarthy, a woman from the crowd climbed into the ring and began pounding McCarthy with one of her high heels. McCarthy needed several stitches and refused to continue the fight, giving Wilson the win. The fan with the dangerous heels was Wilson's mother.

➔ During an on-field celebration following Stevenage's soccer victory over Newcastle, one fan punched out one of his own team's players, Scott Laird. The fan's lawyer told the judge that he did it because his girlfriend used to date Laird and he "had not treated her correctly." After the incident, the fan turned himself in because he was "feeling like a bit of a prat in front of all those people."

➜ A drunken Cleveland Browns fan, angry over his team's loss to the New York Jets at Browns Stadium, took out his frustration by tackling an eight-year-old boy from behind because he was wearing a Jets jersey. The family decided against calling the police, and instead hightailed it out of there. The boy's mother said that Browns fans also threw food at the boy (and his dad) and called him "a bad word." Both teams have reached out to the family and offered free tickets, and in the Jets' case, free transportation and hotel accommodations; however, the family has refused.

➜ A fan ran onto the field just before the final match of the 2010 soccer World Cup and tried to pick up the trophy and put a little red hat on it. The man wore a larger, matching red hat. He got within arm's reach before being punched and tackled to the ground.

SWINDLERS

And now, ladies and gentlemen, I present a special type of law-breaker: those who think they are smarter than the rest of us (or actually *are* smarter than the rest of us). They believe they can beat the system, put one over on us, and run off with all our money. The ones who truly *are* smarter than us do all of that and more . . . since they often get away with it. And then we cheer them on and call them folk heroes. Go figure.

The Welfare King

Anthony Moreno pulled one over on the French social security in Marseilles by forging birth certificates and school registration forms, inventing 197 fake families and three thousand children, all of whom he claimed benefits on in the 1960s. He was never apprehended and moved to Spain to spend his fortune.

Like Eating Glass

A married couple in Boston, Massachusetts, certainly seemed to have really bad luck. Over an eight-year period, they received more than $200,000 in compensation following claims that they were injured in several different incidents after eating food with glass in it. It happened in hotels, restaurants, grocery stores, and more. What are the odds? Well, according to federal prosecutors, not very good, as the couple is now behind bars, convicted of fraud, conspiracy, and more for eating shards of glass on purpose to collect the insurance money. They are both currently serving multiyear prison terms.

Nurse Not-So-Much

Perhaps reading about someone who impersonated a doctor, nurse, or other professional and got away with it for a certain amount of time isn't quite so bizarre anymore, but this one gets a special award for ingenuity. A Connecticut woman who claimed she was a nurse and found gainful employment as a full-time registered nurse at a doctor's office went a step further than most fakers when she created her own nursing organization and then awarded herself the 2008 Nurse of the Year award. More than forty people attended the award ceremony, which cost the woman more than $2,000 to stage. Her boss was a guest speaker. The fifty-six-year-old was finally arrested after a patient complained about her and someone thought to finally fact-check her resume.

Drinking While Not Driving

A Missouri man was acquitted of drunk driving charges after telling the judge that he started drinking after he crashed his car on an icy road. The man reported that after being out with friends late one February evening, he lost control of his car on the slippery highway and landed in a culvert. He then proceeded to drink alcohol in order to keep warm. By the time paramedics arrived at the scene, the man was drunk, but nobody could prove he was drunk before he crashed. He was cleared of all charges.

Killer Voice

A murderer in most Western countries cannot profit from his crime. This apparently is not the case in Indonesia, where serial killer Verry Idham Henyansyah, also known as Ryan, has kept himself quite busy while imprisoned on death row.

In February 2009, he published his tell-all autobiography, *Confessions: The Untold Story of Ryan*. This gruesome account includes maps to the graves of his victims as well as photographs. Then, in May, he released an album of pop tunes called *My Last Performance*. He is visited by hordes of teenage girls who pose for pictures with him in his holding cell, and he, upon request, will sing to reporters and court officers.

In 2008, Ryan was found guilty of murdering and dismembering a man who was interested in Ryan's boyfriend, stuffing the body parts in a suitcase, and then discarding the body along the side of a road. He has also pleaded guilty to murder for the ten bodies found buried in his parent's backyard.

Can he profit from all this? "It is the right of the accused to write a book and make a music album. No problem," said Deputy Attorney

General Abdul Hakim Ritonga. "The accused, like any other artist, also has the right to claim royalties from the sale of book or album. Indonesia does not prohibit that." Talk about an interesting career move!

In October 2010, the openly gay serial killer announced his engagement to Eny Wijaya, a woman he met at the Jakarta Police Narcotics Detention Center, where she was being detained for dealing drugs. "I know I am gay. I don't know if I can keep her happy. But my mother really wants me to marry a woman," Ryan said. Both sets of parents gave their blessing.

Got Change for a Million?

A man from the Ivory Coast was arrested in Abu Dhabi after trying to persuade an employee from the Central Bank of the United Arab Emirates to give him change for two entirely fictional U.S. one-million-dollar bills. The bills featured George Washington's portrait from the U.S. one-dollar bill.

Supermodel Mules

Angela Sanclemente Valencia is a Colombian former lingerie model who found a more lucrative occupation: masterminding one of the world's largest drug gangs using only female models to transport cocaine from South America to Europe and North America. Models would hide the drugs in their baggage as they traveled to photo shoots and beauty competitions. Valencia's "unsuspicious beautiful

angels" (as she is reported to have called her glamour mules) made around $5,000 per trip. Valencia was apprehended (after a two-month manhunt) when one of her models was arrested and started talking.

Doctor Feel Up

A seventy-six-year-old man was arrested and charged with sexually assaulting two women. The man claimed to be a door-to-door doctor from a local hospital who was offering free breast exams. One of the women who initially agreed to an exam became suspicious when the "doctor" told her to remove all her clothing and then didn't put on gloves before attempting to perform a genital exam. She called the cops and the elderly man, who was actually a shuttle driver for an auto dealership, was soon caught at another woman's home.

Man-Boy

Chad Johnson was just a normal fourteen-year-old middle school football player whose parents had died tragically in a car accident. But something seemed a little off with him, and the more Tampa, Florida, authorities dug into this five feet eleven, 160-pound middle schooler, the less things looked normal. Finally the truth came out: The "boy" was actually a twenty-one-year-old man who is now in jail for trespassing on school grounds, obstruction by a disguised person, and violation of probation.

The football coach started getting suspicious when "Johnson" kept his helmet on even after the one game he played for the Town & Country Packers was over. When the coach began investigating, he found a Facebook page that listed the man's mother as well as the high school he graduated from.

"He really acted like a kid," said the coach. "My son is thirteen, and my son was hanging out with him, and he acted more immature than my son." Nobody's quite sure why the man did this, but his coach has a guess. "He just wanted to play football. I don't think he was good enough to play semipro or anything . . . They say he's a man, but he really acted like a sweet kid."

IN OTHER NEWS: Immokalee High School in Collier County, Florida, had sanctions imposed on its sports program when it came to light that a forward for their soccer team, which won district titles in 2005 and 2006, was thirty years old. The local newspaper obtained documents that showed the high school used two other overage athletes as well.

For the Rest of Us

An inmate in Orange County, California, asked for kosher meals to help him stay healthy while incarcerated. Since officials reserve kosher meals for people with religious needs, a judge asked for a reason. The inmate's lawyer said his client was a devotee of Festivus, the holiday that features an aluminum pole and the annual airing of grievances that was created by the TV sitcom *Seinfeld*. The judge granted the request and the inmate got his meals for two months, until a higher court rescinded the previous judge's ruling.

Army Intelligence

A Chinese man in Los Angeles, California, was arrested for creating a fake U.S. Army unit. He convinced more than one hundred Chinese nationals that joining his unit, called the U.S. Army Military Special Forces Reserve unit, would help them gain U.S. citizenship. The "recruits" paid hundreds of dollars to join, received military uniforms, fake documents, and military ID cards. They met regularly in an LA suburb to march and parade around a bit. They could also pay more to their "supreme commander" (as the suspect called himself) for higher ranks within the unit. The suspect has been charged with theft by false pretenses and creating deceptive government documents. He faces up to eight years in jail if found guilty.

Tower of Scrap

In 1925, an Austrian con artist named Victor Lustig read an article in a French newspaper about the high cost of maintaining the Eiffel Tower. The story led to his greatest con. He contacted six scrap metal dealers and, passing himself off as a government official, told the businessmen in strictest confidence that the Eiffel Tower was to be demolished and sold for scrap metal, and the government was soliciting confidential bids to do the work. Lustig picked his mark ahead of time, an insecure dealer named Andre Poisson, and told him he had won the bid to take apart the tower. All was going well with the con and Lustig was just about to close the 250,000 franc deal (nearly $1 million), when Poisson became suspicious. (Legend has it his wife smelled a rat.) Lustig then demanded a bribe from Poisson, which convinced the dealer that all was well because, his thinking went, all French bureaucrats were corrupt. The deal went down and Lustig disappeared with the full amount of the bid as well as the bribe. A humiliated Poisson didn't even contact the police, which gave Lustig the confidence to return to Paris and try again. He selected six more dealers, but this time his mark went to the police before the deal could be completed. Lustig escaped nonetheless.

Flab 'n' Grab

Two obese women in Edmond, Oklahoma, were arrested for using their assets to shoplift at a T.J.Maxx. They were caught stuffing items under their belly fat and breasts. An officer reported that the women were "concealing, eh, um, in the area of their body where excess skin was . . . um . . . underneath their chest area and up in their armpits and things of that nature." (Nice try, officer!) And we're not just talking about scarves and underwear here. One of the women had three boots hidden underneath her breasts. No word on where she hid the fourth one. In fact, all told, police found four pairs of boots, three pairs of jeans, a wallet, and a pair of gloves between different folds of skin—more than $2,500 worth of merchandise.

IN OTHER NEWS: An Indiana teenager was arrested for shoplifting after stuffing her pockets with several items from a local market, including a box of Nestlé Nesquik, a potato peeler, an ice-cream scoop, measuring spoons, six Rollo candy bars, and more. A store employee tried to stop her from running off by grabbing her coat, and she almost got away—that is, until her weighted-down pants fell to her ankles. Cops arrived to an unobstructed view of the woman's bare behind as she tried to back her way out of the store's front door.

THEY JUST COULDN'T TAKE IT ANYMORE

The guy in the next lane cuts you off. You scream. You curse. You threaten the man with bodily harm. But your car windows are closed and nobody can hear you. And that's probably a good thing, since you might set *him* off and he could have a bigger gun than you do. We're a society set to blow at any slight provocation—a powder keg waiting for a spark. And when we do end up losing it and going into a fit of rage, the results are often hard to believe, as our actions, in retrospect, are so out of proportion to the cause.

The Bad Humor Man

A Cape Coral, Florida, man was arrested for threatening the life of the driver of an ice-cream truck. The ice-cream man told police that a quite angry man approached the truck and yelled, "Who told you to come here? Don't come back here or I'll shoot you in the *&@#^$% head." Police confronted the man, who told them that the music coming from the ice-cream truck's speakers was driving him crazy. No arguments there.

Fasten Your Seatbelts

A man on a Southwest Airlines flight from Las Vegas was arrested for punching a fifteen-year-old teenager who refused to turn off his iPhone as the flight prepared to land. The kid was playing a video game on his phone when a flight attendant told passengers to turn off all electronic devices. When the teen failed to comply, the assailant punched him. Officers arrested the man after the plane landed, although he claims he only "tapped" the kid on the arm.

Taxi Rage

A passenger in a taxi in Sacramento, California, became enraged with his driver as they argued over the best way to arrive at his desired destination. He pulled a knife on the cabbie, and the taxi driver ran off. The knife-wielding customer also ran off, but not before leaving the fee and a tip behind.

Nursing Home Crimes

A ninety-eight-year-old woman in Dartmouth, Massachusetts, was charged with second-degree murder for strangling her one-hundred-year-old roommate at the Brandon Woods nursing home. The roommate was found dead with a plastic shopping bag tied around her head. And though it was first thought to be a suicide, an autopsy indicated murder. It was believed that the younger woman was suffering from paranoia and was convinced her roommate "was taking over the room" that they shared. The victim had previously complained that her roommate was making her life "a living hell" and had moved a table to prevent her from using the bathroom. A representative from the nursing home, however, said the two women were good friends who told each other "I love you" each night before going to bed. The accused is most likely the oldest person to face a murder charge in Massachusetts history.

Shooting at the Stars

2010's *Dancing with the Stars* (a television dancing contest) bothered many a fan when the not-quite-so-talented Bristol Palin, daughter of the polarizing vice presidential candidate Sarah Palin, kept not losing. In fact, she made it all the way to the finals (some say because conservative Christians were voting in blocks) before finally losing to Jennifer Grey (Ferris Bueller's sister and Patrick Swayze's Baby in *Dirty Dancing*). While most fans talked about their disbelief and anger around the water cooler at work, one sixty-seven-year-old Madison, Wisconsin, man did something different. After watching Palin dance, the enraged man (who had a history of psychological problems) left the room and returned with his shotgun. He shot the television and then pointed the gun at his wife. She ran to safety and called authorities.

IN OTHER NEWS: A Georgia man got a little upset when he saw actor Charlie Sheen show up unexpectedly on *Jimmy Kimmel Live!* and kiss Jimmy Kimmel. The apparently drunk man snapped and began fighting with his girlfriend, yelling, "I don't want to see that $%&*. I'm not a *&@#^$% gay man." The man got out his gun, waved it around, and aimed it at his girlfriend as well as at neighbors who arrived when they overheard the yelling. Then he made a run for it. He was later tackled and arrested attempting to cross a highway.

The Whistle Whacker

A Framingham, Massachusetts, man was arrested on assault charges after hitting a janitor on the back of the head with a roll of toilet paper. The custodian was whistling while cleaning up the town hall men's room, which apparently irked the man, who was in one of the stalls. He yelled at the custodian about the whistling and then hit him with the toilet paper.

Assault with Deadly Feces

A woman in Belmont, Massachusetts, angry at a motorist who was speeding in the neighborhood, threw a bag of dog poop at the car as it passed, hitting the driver in the face. The woman was charged with assault and battery with a dangerous weapon, vandalism, and disorderly conduct.

Insecurity Cameras

A study in 2008 of security cameras in San Francisco, California, found that crime had indeed gone down . . . as in farther down the street. The study concluded that the effect on crime rates was "incredibly localized," and that although crime went down in front of the cameras, it actually went up down the street from the cameras. The report also stated that "murders went down within 250 feet of the cameras, but the reduction was completely offset by an increase 250 to 500 feet away."

The CSI Effect

Fighting crime is tough enough without your favorite prime-time dramas getting in the way, but some scientists and lawyers are saying that's exactly what's happening. A former chief pathologist in England stated that because of shows such as *CSI: Crime Scene Investigation*, jurors expect more scientific proof that a crime has been committed than forensics is able to deliver. This phenomenon has become known as the "CSI effect." Here are some of the symptoms:

→ Jurors think they know the science of forensics because they saw it on television, even though the shows don't purport to show actual science.

→ Trials are lasting longer, as jurors need to be shown the difference between fact and television before lawyers can even try or defend their cases. The lawyers sometimes even have to hire "negative evidence" witnesses who take the stand to explain what is and isn't real.

→ Defense lawyers, realizing that jurors may believe lack of scientific evidence constitutes reasonable doubt, play it up when defending their clients.

→ Jurors know what a DNA test can do, but don't understand when it is appropriate to use one.

→ Cases that once would have been quick convictions are ending in acquittals.

→ Since these television shows are at least somewhat based on truth, criminals who watch TV are becoming more savvy and using bleach, which destroys DNA, to clean up after themselves. They're also wearing gloves, remembering not to lick envelopes, and more.

Don't Egg Him On

A man from Atlanta, Georgia, enraged that his gold Mercedes had been egged on Halloween, stopped his car, confronted the seventeen-year-old egger, and then shot the teen ten times, killing him.

CRIME STOPPERS

When a bad guy does a bad thing, he or she needs to be apprehended. Civilization is nothing if not the ability to catch the bad guys so the good guys can leave their car doors open when they pop into a Starbucks for their daily Frappuccino. We've come up with all sorts of systems to catch and prosecute the wrongdoers; however, sometimes we need to think outside the box to get the job done. We as a society need to get a little creative at times. And we do, often to hilarious results. When the system fails, we as individual citizens often take the law into our own hands. If that means donning spandex tights and a mask, so be it.

Life in New York

Published in 1886, *Danger! A True History of a Great City's Wiles and Temptations: The Veil Lifted, and Light Thrown on Crime and its Causes, and Criminals and their Haunts. Facts and Disclosures* purports to teach the fine citizens of New York how to avoid getting robbed. How nice! Upon closer inspection, however, the book didn't teach innocents how to fight crime, but instead taught unsavory types how to commit just about any crime imaginable. Including blackmail, breaking and entering, cracking safes, shoplifting, thwarting the court system, murder, and more, this book covers it all. It was an instant best seller and required reading for New York's most unsavory characters.

HERE'S A SAMPLE: Before leaving home on a thieving excursion to the stores the female shop-lifter carefully and systematically prepares her clothing, and sees that it is in proper form and ready for business. This she does by first putting on a corset made especially for the purpose, with broad, strong bands which pass over the shoulders. Between her legs she arranges a large bag or receptacle made of some extremely strong cloth, which is suspended from the corset by a stout band running around the waist. Her dress or frock covers this, and in front of the dress is an opening or slit, nicely arranged in the folds so as not to be noticed, which leads into the suspended bag. Over this, in winter, is worn a sealskin sacque, cloth cloak, fur circular, or other garment, according to the means of the wearer. In summer she wears a light shawl, which completely hides the slit in the dress from view. She now takes her muff, which, to the uninitiated eye, has nothing to distinguish it, outwardly, from thousands of other muffs, but which is a master-piece of ingenious contrivance. It is covered with any kind of fur, just as honest muffs are, with the significant exception that, instead of being padded with cotton, the fur rests upon a framework of wire. Between the fur covering and the wire supporting frame, the space usually filled with cotton is left vacant, thus providing accommodation for quite a stock of valuable lace, articles of jewelry, gloves, or anything small and valuable . . . Thus equipped, the expert female shop-lifter sallies out . . .

Asking the saleswoman to be shown some kinds of lace, she examines it critically, and, laying it down upon the counter, asks to see another kind, or some feathers, or something else, and so contrives to have several articles just before her, one covering the other, if possible. Having accumulated a number of articles upon the counter in an eligible position, she points to some things high up on a shelf behind the counter, thus getting the saleswoman's back turned towards her for an instant, when, with soft dexterity, she conveys anything that happens to be handily in the way through the slit in her dress into the bag between her legs. The goods examined and priced, "not suiting" her, and other customers coming up, she takes the opportunity of moving to another counter, where the same tactics are repeated, and so on, till she is satisfied with her haul or exhausted her stowage capacity.

As you can see, although presented as information for crime *stoppers*, there's way too much information here—a plethora of information for the entrepreneurial shoplifter! You can download this tremendous tome at http://www.gutenberg.org/ebooks/24717.

Would You Like a Receipt with That?

A bank in South Africa has devised an ingenious way of deterring ATM theft. Absa Bank, responding to the rash of cash machines being tampered with and blown up with explosives, decided to arm the ATMs with pepper spray. A machine detects when an ATM is being tampered with and then ejects pepper spray to "stun the culprit while police response teams race to the scene." Needless to say, not all is going according to plan. A spokesperson for the bank said, "During a routine maintenance check . . . the pepper spray device was accidentally activated." The technicians working on the machine required treatment from paramedics. I'm not sure if the pepper spray devices can handle such evasive maneuvers from would-be ATM thieves as gas masks and ducking, though.

The Rain City Superheroes

In January 2011, a man in Seattle, Washington, was in the middle of getting carjacked when suddenly, "From the right, this guy comes dashing in, wearing this skintight rubber, black-and-gold suit, and starts chasing [the would-be crook] away." As surprising as it was for the fortunate man, it's just another day at the office for Phoenix Jones, the Guardian of Seattle, a real-life superhero. For more than a year, Phoenix and his team (yes, he has his own version of the Justice League called the Rain City Superhero Movement, with a sidekick named Buster Doe and colleagues who go by the names Thorn, Green Reaper, Gemini, No Name, Catastrophe, Thunder 88, and more) have been patrolling the streets of Seattle at night. Phoenix and his cohorts do not have superpowers, nor do they do anything illegal. But, if they see something going down, they intervene.

Phoenix's costume includes blue tights, black cape, black fedora, white belt and mask, body armor, ballistic vest, and arm and leg trauma plates. He and his friends carry Tasers, nightsticks, and pepper spray. So far, Seattle's police department has worked with the superheroes, albeit reluctantly. They would rather the heroes act as good witnesses than put themselves at risk.

Want to become a real superhero? The Rain City Superheroes are part of a national movement of self-described superheroes who are beginning to pop up in major U.S. cities. There's even a website for those who wish to become a superhero. The site, www.rlsh-manual. com, states that "A Real Life Superhero is whoever chooses to embody the values presented in superheroic comic books, not only by donning a mask/costume, but also performing good deeds for the communitarian place whom he inhabits." But just because you don a pair of tights, don't think you'll automatically be invited to all the superhero meetings. Phoenix said, "I don't condone people walking around on the street with masks. Everyone on my team either has a military background or a mixed martial arts background, and we're well aware of what it costs to do what we do."

You can watch Phoenix on YouTube talking about getting his nose broken while trying to break up a fight. While holding one guy in a headlock, another person held a gun to Phoenix, who ended up getting kicked in the face. But not to worry; Phoenix Jones is not easily deterred! He's back on the street fighting crime.

Senior Moments

Note to the bad guys: Think twice before attempting to rob or otherwise harm the elderly. They may just kick your ass.

→ A naked ninety-one-year-old Lake Worth, Florida, man held a twenty-six-year-old burglar at gunpoint until police arrived.

→ Another burglar trying to rob an elderly man wasn't so lucky. The twenty-four-year-old broke into a home waving a toy gun and was shot and killed by an eighty-two-year-old homeowner with the real thing.

→ Meanwhile, a grandmother in Northampton, England, has been nicknamed "Super Granny" after she approached a gang of robbers who were trying to smash into a jewelry store window and started hitting them with her pocketbook. An employee at the store said, "We were terrified. We locked the door. We hid under the desk . . . And then, we looked outside, and, God love her, she was running down the road, with her handbag in the air, banging them on the back of their helmet with her handbag." The would-be crooks tried to escape on their scooters, but most of them were caught.

→ An eighty-eight-year-old woman in Mayfield, Kentucky, upon seeing an intruder wearing a pumpkin mask in her home, asked who he was and what he was doing there. The man wrestled her into the bedroom and tried to smother her with a pillow. The octogenarian, who was "mad enough to do almost anything," kicked him in "a vital spot," forcing him to flee.

Batter Up

A woman who was being assaulted by an old boyfriend with a gun was rescued by her eight-year-old son and his friend when they attacked the man with baseball bats. The man ran off and was soon captured.

The Guac Cops

In January 2004, a special squad of San Diego, California, police officers was formed to combat a serious crime in the area that always seems to spike just before the Super Bowl. These cops specialize in catching avocado thieves from ripping off local growers. Even though sellers need documentation to sell green gold (as avocados are known in the area), authorities report that it's easy to launder the fruit, and with the Super Bowl being the biggest dip day of the year, the Guac Cops were called into action. They track thieves, hide in trees, and go undercover in order to protect the trees that provide nearly 70 percent of the nation's avocados. "It's like identity theft," said one of the Guac Cops. "The problem is, when God made avocados, he didn't put serial numbers on them."

Knew I Was Forgetting Something

In 2008, a thirty-eight-year-old Arkansas woman got caught up in a CD-bootlegging sting operation at a local flea market and was arrested. When she showed up at court on a Thursday to plead innocent to the charges, the bailiff locked her up, and then promptly forgot about her for four days. Left in a tiny room that had only a metal table, two benches, and a light that never turned off, the woman had nothing to eat or drink and nowhere to go to the bathroom. Afraid she was going to die, she resorted to drinking her urine between bouts of banging on the door. Unfortunately, it snowed on Friday, so there wasn't much staff around, and then the courthouse was closed all weekend. Unsurprisingly, all charges against the woman were eventually dropped. After serving a suspension for forgetting about the woman, the bailiff has returned to work. No word yet on the lawsuit.

Going the Extra Mile

A Lawrenceville, Georgia, sheriff's deputy was commended for finding a loaded pistol that a nineteen-year-old suspect nearly smuggled into the Gwinnett County jail. He found the gun hidden between the man's buttocks. "We are proud that our deputy was diligent in his job and was able to locate the weapon," the sheriff's spokesperson said.

If the Shoes Fit

A Riceville, Tennessee, man whose house had been robbed was talking to a detective outside his home when another officer stopped a passerby. The homeowner noticed that the man the detective had stopped was wearing his stolen pants and shoes. Detectives arrested the thief and the homeowner got his clothes back.

The Wrong Kind of Advertising

What happens when you steal thousands of dollars worth of electrical gear from a billboard company? Well, if you happened to rob OTW, an advertising firm in Auckland, New Zealand, (and you're unlucky enough to have your picture taken by a suspicious passerby) you'd get your picture on four billboards around the city. The company erected the billboards showing a clear picture of the man walking off with the stolen goods and a catchy slogan: "Who is this thief? Reward $500." The owner of the firm stated, "It's a crime that has a big impact on our company . . . We felt obligated to say 'right, can we match this guy's face to a name?'"

He Urned it

The armed man probably wasn't all that concerned at first when a female employee of the Morristown, Tennessee, funeral home he was
attempting to rob walked in on him. That was before she:

1. struck him in the back of the head with an urn,
2. threw a chair at him, and
3. hit him again with more urns.

The man "staggered" away from the funeral home with some cash
and a story best kept to himself.

GREAT ESCAPES

And finally, for the criminal mind who wants to get away from it all (if "all" is to be defined as "jail" or "the scene of the crime"), here is a selection of great, almost great, and not so great escapes.

Just Think of the Splinters

Four out of five dentists don't recommend escaping from jail this way: In the early twentieth century, Hans Schaarschmidt was serving a six-year sentence for robbery in the decaying German jail in Gera. The windows were barred with wooden beams, so each day, Schaarschmidt chewed away at the wooden bars. He hid his handiwork by filling the holes with a paste he made from the black bread he was fed. After three months, he squeezed his way to freedom. He was caught again within three weeks and put behind iron bars.

The Fax Escape Man

A man in Madrid, Spain, has escaped from jail twice via fax. The man was in a cell at the Arganda del Rey courthouse awaiting trial when officers received a faxed release order from a regional court. When the fax was followed up by two phone calls, they release the man to a waiting taxi. The fax and both phone calls were from the man's wife. The husband and wife team had done the same thing successfully six months earlier. Police found the man inside his heavily fortified home, hiding inside a hollowed-out couch.

Naked Escape

A Phoenix, Arizona, man tried to escape from Durango Jail by climbing the five fences meant to keep the bad guys in. He successfully scaled all the fences, although he lost all his clothes to razor wire by the time he was on the other side. All that was left on his person was a pair of pink socks. He was treated for scrapes and bruises and returned to the jail, where he now faces an additional five years for attempted escape.

No Good Deed Goes Unpunished

A twenty-six-year-old Janesville, Minnesota, man was just doing a good deed. Unfortunately, the seventy-year-old woman he was giving a lift to wasn't. He thought he was giving her a ride to the bank so she could withdraw some money to pay the rent. Instead, the woman told a teller she had a gun and demanded money. She left with $3,700 and got back in the car with the unsuspecting getaway driver. Police arrested both soon after (the bank's vice president followed the car for about eight miles), but the driver was released when he explained that he had no idea what that nice little old lady was up to.

Avoiding Jury Duty

A twenty-one-year-old Columbus, Ohio, man had to spend a night in jail after writing on a questionnaire for potential jurors that he was a heroin addict and had killed someone. When asked about using drugs, he said he had a "bad jonesin' for heroin." Had he ever fired a weapon? "Yes. I killed someone with it, of course. Right." He was charged with contempt of court and obstruction of justice. He admitted to lying under oath and apologized for his actions. And best of all, the judge dropped the charges against him and then removed him from the jury pool. I'd call that mission a success!

Grave Consequences

A nineteen-year-old Philadelphia, Pennsylvania, woman who was being transported to jail was able to escape from her captors and run away. It took several hours to reapprehend the handcuffed criminal, who was finally found at the Brown Funeral Home, hiding inside a coffin.

Hide-and-Maul

A mugger in Bloemfontein, South Africa, fleeing from security officers, climbed into a tiger enclosure at the zoo. His dead, mauled, but uneaten, body (the tigers had just been fed) was discovered by a visitor the following day.

Oops, Wrong Car

The plan was to grab a purse from a woman and then get into a friend's car for a quick getaway. And all went well for the East Wenatchee, Washington, purse snatcher as he ran off with the goods toward the car. Unfortunately for him, he was actually running straight for a cop car. The officer stopped the man before he could enter the vehicle.

IN OTHER NEWS: An Ohio man who robbed a bank had his six-year-old daughter in his getaway car. Family friends reported that the girl later said, "I was wondering why my dad was driving so fast."

Taking the Tube

A twenty-eight-year-old man in Monroe, Washington, whose family was having financial problems and whose wife had just given birth, came up with an elaborate armored car heist and getaway. And get away he nearly did. First, he placed an ad on Craigslist calling for workers to show up near the Bank of America around the time of his planned robbery. They were to wear a yellow vest, safety goggles, a respirator mask, and a blue shirt. The job would pay them $28.50 an hour, and about a dozen men showed up. Meanwhile, as the men were milling around outside the bank, the thief, dressed in the same outfit, walked up to a guard who was unloading cash from an armored truck, doused him with pepper spray, and walked off with a bag of loot. The "workers" were simply decoys to throw off the cops. The robber then escaped by riding a rubber inner tube down a creek.

Even after all that effort, the man was eventually caught when police uncovered a report from three weeks prior to the robbery. A homeless man had called the cops after seeing someone behind the same Bank of America recover a wig, safety vest, can of pepper spray, and other items. (The robber was just completing a dry run of his planned heist.) The homeless man also had another piece of evidence: a license plate number, which police used to track down and arrest the thief.

Cigarette Run

A man serving time in jail over driving with a suspended license was upset when an acquaintance didn't show up outside the prison to throw some cigarettes over the fence for him. So he did what anyone would do under these circumstances: He broke out of the Camden County Jail in Woodbine, Georgia, by scaling the fence, broke into a convenience store, grabbed the much-needed cigarettes, and then . . . returned to jail. He was rearrested on the spot and charged with burglary and attempted escape.

The Three Stooges

Three handcuffed men in Ontario, Canada, who were being transported by police officers, decided to make a run for it. They got about half a block before two of the men ran to the left of a pole, while the third man ran to the right of it. The men clotheslined into one another violently. One laughing police officer nailed the situation perfectly as he approached the tangled and bloodied men when he said, "You guys are idiots."

INDEX